The Irish Theologi~~~ __

A NEW AGE OF THE SPIRIT?

A CATHOLIC RESPONSE

to

THE NEW AGE PHENOMENON

VERITAS

First published 1994 by
Veritas Publications
7-8 Lower Abbey Street
Dublin 1

Copyright © The Irish Theological Commission 1994

ISBN 1 85390 237 3

Cover design by Banahan McManus
Printed in the Republic of Ireland by Paceprint Ltd

CONTENTS

INTRODUCTION

The New Age is a Challenge to the Church

This distressed, restless generation is challenging the Church to communicate the Gospel of salvation in a more complete and effective manner. The very presence and success of the so-called New Age Movement is evidence that not all Christians are hearing the Gospel in a life-giving and fruitful way. The New Age challenges the Church to look at the way she serves people. Does she just support those in trouble or does she actually try to transform them? Does she show by her activities that she knows the way for those who have lost it? For she must reasonably expect that if she does not meet the real needs of believers people will go outside the Church. This is demonstrated by the fact that many are turning to new ways to get help and are finding that 'The New World Servers' are only too willing to respond.

The popularity of the New Age represents a great cry from the human heart for inwardness, for an authentic spiritual life, and for a greater sense of purpose in life. To meet these needs the Church offers the Gospel of Jesus Christ. It recognises that not everything in the New Age is evil or bad. The concern for a healthy lifestyle and a healthy environment is good. The desire to live a spiritual life instead of empty materialism is good. The search to understand the workings of our minds, the desire to serve others, both individuals, groups and nations, and to transform this planet into a friendly, cooperative society is good. The desire to heal the environment and to heal the planet itself is good. But these powerful purposes are enshrined also in the gospel of Jesus Christ which is committed to recognising the transforming grace of Christ active in the world. The Christian vision sees, however, that the transformation must not only aim at the better but at the truth and must always contend with the reality of sin, which Christ came to overcome. The Church, then, in function of the truth committed to it, must help people discern the inadequacies and the incompleteness of the New Age response and point to the elements in it

5

which are destructive of the truth of the human situation seen in the light of Christian faith and practice.

The Second Vatican Council, arguably the greatest religious event of this century, had as a primary goal the proclamation of Jesus Christ as the good news of salvation for the modern world. The Council wanted all our contemporaries to hear the full message of salvation 'so that by hearing the message of salvation the whole world may believe, by believing, it may hope, and by hoping, it may love' (*Dei Verbum* 1). The main aim of the Council was to direct the energies of the Church towards a civilisation and culture centred on the love God has for the world he has created. The Council hoped that the world of our time would enter into a way of life inspired by the Spirit of Christ. It invited the Church to go into the world and the world to find its home in the Church.

This explains the positive pastoral tone of the Council and the agenda it set for itself at the end of the second millennium. The fathers of the Council had a childlike certainty that the substance of Christian revelation generates faith, provides the stimulus for hope and ignites the love of God in human hearts and among human hearts. The 'civilisation of love' for which all recent popes have called would require the imaginative and appropriate communication of the riches of the revealed Word which is summed up in Christ, its 'mediator and fullness' (*Dei Verbum* 2). He is the eternal 'life which was with the Father and has been made visible to us' (I Jn 1:2) so that 'you may have fellowship with us; And our fellowship is with the Father and with his Son, Jesus Christ' (v.3).

In practice, however, the truth is that ignorance, misunderstanding and even, at times, plain misrepresentation, threaten to drive the gladness from the glad tidings. Conscious of the never-ending threat, the Council set in motion, some thirty years ago, a process of *aggiornamento*, a great surge of the Holy Spirit, to scatter the divinely fresh seed of the Gospel on the soil of contemporary culture. The Holy Spirit, the very 'soul of the Church', invited the Church to renew itself and bring the Gospel to bear on the aspirations of the people of the world.

The document you are about to read desires to bring this vision to bear on the so-called New Age movement. It follows the methods

6

of St Irenaeus of Lyons (*circa* 130-200 AD), one of the first Christians who faced the problem posed to the Church by the subtle system called 'gnosticism'. The approach of Irenaeus was to exhibit 'the unfathomable riches of Christ' (Ep 3:8), and then refute the encircling errors.

Accordingly, we shall begin with chapters on the Christian understanding of prayer and forgiveness. In doing so we would hope to let the radiant fullness of Catholic faith speak for itself. Subsequently we will provide a statement of the central tenets of the New Age and an outline of the questions most frequently asked about the New Age.

1

CHRISTIAN PRAYER: ITS ORIGINALITY AND LIBERATING POWER

At the very heart of our faith lies the fact that God has come out of his Mystery and revealed himself to us in order to draw us into a new life, and a new world. In Jeremiah 31:3 we read: 'I have loved you with an everlasting love, and so am consistent in my affection for you'. This divine approach to humanity has a long history, one which began with Abraham, the person through whom God wished to bless all the nations of the earth.[1]

This story of God-with-us[2] unfolds through the pages of the Old Testament, where the children of Abraham became the Chosen People, who were given 'the glory and the covenants', as Paul says in Romans 9:4. God manifested himself to them by words and deeds, as the One, True and Living God. The result of this was that 'Israel came to know by experience the ways of God with men'.[3]

For her part Israel discovered that she was God's chosen one, his beloved.[4] The Israelites realised that they were unique persons, each a 'you' addressed by the God of Abraham, Isaac and Jacob. Each one had the chance of hearing these words of Isaiah 43:1,3-4:

> Do not be afraid, for I have redeemed you:
> I have called you by your name, you are mine:
> I give Egypt for your ransom,
> And exchange Cush and Seba for you.
> Because you are precious in my eyes,
> Because you are honoured and I love you.

Since God took the initiative in calling Israel to be his own people, Israel responded with praise and adoration. She became a people of prayer and worship. This is attested to in the Book of Psalms, which grew out of her continued response to God in prayer. These prayers respond to God's creative and saving love. Here are some examples:

> Give thanks to the Lord for he is good,
> His love is everlasting!
> He led his people through the wilderness,
> His love is everlasting!
> He remembered us when we were down,
> His love is everlasting! (Ps 136: 1, 16, 23)

God's love for Israel not only made her into a great nation, but also guided her throughout her history. It made it possible for her to respond to God with love and service, and thus she became a people of prayer, worship and service. Just as a mother's love for her infant eventually evokes the child's smile of recognition, so God's love for Israel called forth the prayer of Israel. To pray is to say 'yes' to God's love for us.

God speaks to us by revealing himself, and our response to that revelation is prayer. The revelation of God in the Old Testament is incomplete, like an unfinished symphony, for God revealed himself in so far as the people could respond. The Prophets saw this clearly. Hosea said that the more God called the people, 'the further they went from him'.[5] God complained through Isaiah, 'I reared sons, I brought them up, but they have rebelled against me.... Israel knows nothing, my people understand nothing.'[6]

The Prophets understood the difficulty of bonding the people to God. This people seemed incapable of living in intimacy with God, and this inability thwarted God's plan for the Covenant, whereby they were to be the people through whom he would set up the kingdom of God on earth. But God is the eternal optimist, and promised to give his people a new and eternal Covenant.[7] And so, in the fullness of time, the eternal Son of God became flesh, 'taking on what he was not, not losing what he is' as St Augustine said. Jesus is the revelation of the invisible God,[8] who speaks to us out of the abundance of his love, makes us his friends, and lives among us, so that he might invite us into fellowship with himself.[9] Jesus, the eternal Word, who is God,[10] not only

9

took on our full human nature, our flesh, he also took on our human condition with its horrific baggage of sin.

In order to accomplish his mission, Jesus sent us his Holy Spirit. It was the Holy Spirit who convinced the Apostles of the Resurrection, and who reminded the disciples of all that the Father and Jesus had done, the one who brought them 'the fullness of grace'.[11] It is little wonder that the sending of the Holy Spirit at Pentecost was the catalyst of prayer.[12] It seems that the outpouring of the Holy Spirit, the 'Lord and Giver of Life', had enabled the disciples to perceive something of the wonder and vastness of the descent of the eternal and only-begotten Son into our history.

The descent of God into our human flesh brings about the ascent of our human flesh into God. St Paul, himself converted to the Crucified and Risen Christ, prays that the believers in Ephesus might be enabled by God the Father to grasp this revelation in order to appreciate the hope that God's call holds for us, and how infinitely great is the power he has exercised for us.[13] Through Christ all believers have access to the Father in the Holy Spirit.[14]

'Christian prayer is always determined by the structure of the Christian faith in which the very truth of God and creatures shines forth'.[15] From what we have been saying it should now be clear that 'there exists a strict relationship between revelation and prayer'.[16] This relationship consists in the fact that God's loving self-communication stimulates and calls forth a response from us that includes prayer. Since God's love reached the heights of handing over to us his Beloved Son 'even unto death on a cross', this raises our humanity to the glory of being at the right hand of the Father.[17]

Christ is the key to prayer, because prayer is all about communion with God, and Jesus is that divine and human communion in its highest form. The only prayer that is authentically Christian is that which rises to God through Christ and the Holy Spirit. St Augustine explains that 'God first praised himself in order to show us how to praise him worthily; and since he has deigned to praise himself, man has discerned how to praise him'.[18]

10

Seven characteristics of Christian Prayer

The full circle of revealed truth opens up stupendous vistas for the prayer-life of believers. First, the prayer-life of the believer has to be inserted into the Trinitarian movement of God, now that God has descended in his Son, and in the Holy Spirit, has lifted up fallen human beings. Whenever Christians pray, be it in the liturgy or in private, or with others, their prayer participates in the praying of Christ who lives to intercede for us,[19] and who commands us to pray always.[20]

Next, we can better appreciate the full sense of the 'our Father' which Jesus gave us in response to a request of his Apostles. This central Christian prayer 'clearly indicates the unity of this movement: the Will of the Father must be done on earth as it is in Heaven. The petitions for bread, forgiveness and protection express the fundamental aspects of God's will for us, so that there may be a new earth in the Heavenly Jerusalem'.[21]

Thirdly, Christians enter through prayer into the life that was made visible when the life-giving Word became flesh.[22] Prayer is necessary for salvation, which consists in taking possession of the spiritual life our Saviour won for us. 'By the mystery of this water and wine, may we come to share in the divinity of Christ who humbled himself to share in our humanity', the priest says daily in the Eucharist. The sheer necessity of prayer becomes evident when we observe the concrete reality of our lives in the world, with its personal and collective dangers.

Cardinal Newman makes the point with great insight: 'We often hear it said that the true way of serving God is to serve man, as if religion consisted merely in acting well our part in life, not in direct faith, obedience and worship. How different is the spirit of this prayer! Evil round about him, enemies and persecutors in his path, temptation in prospect, help for the day, sin to be expiated, God's will in his heart, God's name on his lips, God's kingdom in his hopes: this is the view it gives us of a Christian'.[23]

Fourthly, it is the simple faith of Catholics that our Saviour perpetuated the mystery of his descent from heaven in self-emptying love, and his ascent in glorification as Lord of history, by and in the sacrament of the Eucharist. 'Every time you eat this bread and drink this cup you proclaim the Lord's death until he comes'.[24] The Liturgy of the Eucharist encapsulates and hands on forever the prayer of Christ offered up with loud cries.[25] The Holy Eucharist as the sacrament of the Lord's death and resurrection gathers up the whole of life in its greatness and littleness, in its joy and sorrow, and plunges it into the dying and restoring Christ.

Fifthly, Christians who are faithful to prayer grow in the love of God, the Holy Trinity, and so reach the fullness of their self-identity. Christ, in fact, is the true measure of our existence, and the key to the mystery of our humanity, whose greatness he reveals in our capacity for God. In him we discern what it means to be created for God who is love.

Moreover, when we pray, we may do so either merely as creatures of the Creator, or as children of the Father through Baptism.[26] As creatures, our prayer is weak, and we are far from God. As children, our prayer is strong and intimate, for it is the prayer to our Father who loves us. How wonderful! We can call the Father of our Lord, Jesus Christ, 'Abba', 'Daddy', 'Dearest Father', because we are in his Son, and therefore share in his relationship to the Father. We are sons and daughters in 'the only-begotten Son'.

Furthermore, prayer is not only an individual thing: it is also an activity of remarkable social implications. Since by Baptism we are all incorporated into the Body of Christ,[27] and have all drunk the same spirit, the prayer of each one of us has its bearing on the well-being of others.[28] Prayer may be intensely personal in its performance and that even in the case of liturgical prayer, but its performance and fruits are socially powerful. An aspect of this is the 'prayer of unity': 'I tell you most solemnly, if two of you on earth agree to ask anything at all, it will be granted to you by my Father in Heaven'.[29]

In order to pray better, some people have recourse to various methods or techniques. Church history records a rich legacy of method, and of the experience of prayer. A new phenomenon has emerged today, however, in the form of psychological-corporal methods. Since, 'in prayer it is the whole man who must enter into relation with God, and so his body should also take up the position most suited to recollection',[30] Christians today, therefore, are becoming more conscious of how our bodily posture can help in prayer. Some disquiet arises where certain preparatory exercises, sometimes imported from non-Christian religions, are employed without discernment. Perhaps two principles should enable us to discern what is good and to hold fast to that: first, the essential Christian and Trinitarian character of prayer must be maintained; second, techniques of relaxation are only means to prayer: they are emphatically not prayer.

Prayer is more necessary to the soul than food is to the body. Prayer is, in fact, the oxygen of the soul. Since God is the life of the soul, and since he seeks communion with us,[31] we must cultivate this first and most basic of all relationships, without which we do not reach our destiny as people or as Christians. The gospel tells us to pray constantly.[32] This does not mean to recite prayers always. Rather it means to say 'yes' to God's holy will in our daily lives with the help of his saving grace. The daily duties of our life can all become an abiding prayer provided we set the compass towards the magnetic north of God's will. 'Whether you eat or drink or sleep, do all in the name of our Lord Jesus Christ'.

Since the purpose of prayer is not in itself, but in building up friendship with God through Jesus and in the Holy Spirit, doing the will of God well in the present moment[33] turns our day into a lasting prayer. To achieve this, however, we need to be able to cope and to live with the daily trials and hardships. We need to see in these sufferings the face of Jesus, 'despised and the most abject of men, a man of sorrows and familiar with grief'.[34]

NOTES

1.   Genesis 12:3
2.   Isaiah 7:14
3.   *Dei Verbum* 14
4.   See Deuteronomy 7:7f; Hosea 11:1f
5.   Hosea 11:2
6.   Isaiah 1:2-3
7.   See Jeremiah 31:31f; I Cor 11:25

8.   Colossians 1:15; I Timothy 1:17
9.   See Exodus 33:11; John 15:14-15; Baruch 3:38; *DV* 2
10.   John 1:1
11.   Eucharistic Prayer IV.
12.   See Acts 4:24-30; 6:4; 2:42, 46; 12:5, 12 etc.
13.   Ephesians 1:18
14.   See Ephesians 2:18; *DV* 2; LG 4
15.   *Christian Meditation*: Letter to Bishops on some aspects of Meditation: CDF 1990 S3
16.   Ibid., 15
17.   Philippians 2:8, 11.
18.   Quoted in Pius X, *Divino Afflatu*, AAS 3 (1911) 633
19.   Hebrews 7:25
20.   Luke 18:1
21.   CDF 7
22.   I John 1:2; John 1:14,17
23.   *Sermons on Subjects of the Day*, 289
24.   I Corinthians 11:26
25.   Luke 15:37; Hebrews 5:7; *SC* 47
26.   See Galatians 4:4-7; Romans 8:15-17
27.   Romans 6:3; Galatians 3:27
28.   Romans 14:7
29.   Matthew 18:19
30.   CDF 26
31.   I John 1:1-4; John 15:1-17
32.   Luke 18:1
33.   See Matthew 7:21
34.   Isaiah 53:3

2

THE GOOD NEWS OF GOD'S FORGIVENESS

Some people find it difficult to believe in God's love for the individual, and to realise that he calls each one personally. Many find difficulty in believing that God's Providence covers the whole of their life. Yet God takes care of the birds of the air and the lilies of the field. Indeed, world events, and the cruel, tragic experiences of individuals, groups, and even whole nations, often blind us to the reality of the presence of our Creator in his handiwork. The human condition is laden with pain as well as joy, suffering as well as contentment, conflict as well as peace. Many of these ills seem to be a direct result of our own disordered choices, while others, such as natural disasters, cannot be traced easily to human wrongdoing.

The Second Vatican Council considers these ills in depth, and lists the inescapable questions to which they give rise. 'What is the human being? What is the meaning and purpose of our life? What is goodness and what is sin? What gives rise to our sorrows, and to what intent? Where lies the path to true happiness?'.[1] It is true, of course, that our age is also an age of impressive scientific, social and technological progress. Humanity has extended its control over nature, and one could see in that a fulfilment of the command God gave us 'to subdue the earth' (Gn 1:28). It is most certainly true that the benefits of these achievements have alleviated considerably many of the maladies afflicting people. 'Now for the first time in history people are not afraid to think that cultural benefits are for all, and should be available to everybody'.[2] Sadly, the greater part of the human family has so far had little or no access to these benefits. This only increases the aspirations of people to share in the goods of modern civilisation.

The grandeur and misery

The broad aspirations of contemporary people towards a fuller and more human life are continually contradicted by the negative experience of evil and failure, whether personal or social. To take but

15

one example, this century of astounding scientific progress is also the century of wars unparalleled in the history of the world. Since the end of World War Two more than sixteen million people have died in bloody conflict. What is the meaning of this dichotomy affecting the modern world? It 'is, in fact, a symptom of a deeper dichotomy that is in man himself. He is a meeting point of many conflicting forces. In his condition as a created being he is subject to a thousand shortcomings, but feels untrammelled in his inclinations and destined for a higher form of life'.[3] This is what Pascal meant by the 'grandeur' and 'misery' of the human condition, or what Cardinal Newman meant by its 'greatness' and 'littleness'. Worse still, feeble as they are, human beings often do the very thing they hate and do not do what they want. They sin.

The human condition, then, is one of bewildering ambiguity: of hope challenged by despair, of greatness contradicted by moral misery. Any plan of salvation would have to match this vision of the world that both shocks and appals. It would have to encompass and fulfil both our grandeur of aspiration and our frequently miserable performance. Now this is precisely the shape and form of our Catholic faith.

At its core lies the person of Jesus Christ who both endured the greatest suffering ('Oh! all you who pass by, look and see if there is any suffering like mine' (Lm 1:12)), and entered the greatest glory (see Phil 2:9-10). One and the same person encompasses and enfolds the reality of suffering and love. In doing so he brings together and overcomes radical opposites. That is why he is the only name in Heaven or earth who can save us (Ac 4.12).

The programme of Jesus of Nazareth

In the synagogue of Nazareth 'where he had been brought up' (Lk 4:16) Jesus read from the prophet Isaiah: 'The Spirit of the Lord is upon me, for he has anointed me to bring good news to the poor...' (Lk 4:18ff). His subsequent ministry was the living out of this programme (Ac 1:1). He cured the sick, as in the cases of Simon's mother-in-law (Lk 4:38-39) and the man covered with leprosy (Lk 5:12-14). He drew the sinner, Levi, out of a world of selfishness and into a life of generosity (Lk 5:27-32). He forgave the sins of 'the

16

woman with the bad name' and praised her great love, identifying it as the fruit of the forgiveness of 'her sins, her many sins' (Lk 7:36-50). He cast out devils from the possessed (Lk 4:33-37; 8:26-39; 11:14-22).

Finally, he unmasked 'the spoilt religion' of the pharisees and the lawyers, who neglected justice, mercy and the love of God, while laying heavy burdens on the shoulders of the people (Lk 11:37-54). The people around Jesus were often broken, sick, and far from God's Kingdom. Many were locked into the slavery of sin, far from the attitude of respect and reverence for others which constitutes the second commandment. For each and every one of these people Jesus was good news. He was the good news that brought liberty to those caught in the tyranny of sin. He was sight to those blind to the meaning of life, hope to the broken-hearted, and the divine favour of forgiveness for those weighed down by guilt.

In Jesus, the Father's eternal merciful love met the misery and need of the people, as well as their craving for freedom and reconciliation. The result was that 'the tax-collectors and sinners were all seeking his company to hear what he had to say' (Lk 15:1). He convinced them by his person, by his deeds and by his words that 'there is more joy in Heaven over one repentant sinner than over ninety-nine virtuous men who have no need of repentance' (Lk 15:7).

The truth is that, in his face, everyone caught the reflection of the Father of mercies (II Co 1:3) as Luke's Gospel so splendidly illustrates from beginning to end. As the only Son of the Father, and the one nearest his heart, Jesus interpreted, made present and communicated to us the grace and truth of his Father (Jn 1:16,18). Jesus is, in fact, the Father's perfect self-portrait: whoever sees Jesus sees the Father (Jn 14:9).

In his encyclical *Dives in misericordia*, Pope John Paul II writes: 'Not only does Jesus speak of mercy and explain it by the use of comparisons and parables, but above all he himself makes it incarnate and personifies it. He himself, in a certain sense, *is* Mercy. To the person who sees it in him – and finds it in him – God becomes visible in a particular way as the Father "who is rich in mercy" (Ep 2:4; *DM* 2)'. In that way God makes himself known in the way

17

most people need to know him, as a holy and yet most merciful Saviour.

Jesus Crucified: The Revelation of the Father's Mercy and the Proof of the Love of the Trinity for the World

In the agony in Gethsemane a dramatic change occurred in our Lord and in his Mission. The burden of sin was laid upon him, and he felt it in an indescribable way, so that 'a sudden fear came over him, and great distress' (Mk 14:34). The terrible chalice of his Passion, Cross and engagement with 'the powers of darkness' was before him. He chose to drink the chalice filled with all the 'No's' of sinners to the Father's Will: 'Your Will be done, not mine' (Mk 14:36).

In his Passion Christ entered into the greatest possible solidarity with sinners. And because he did this 'God laid upon him the sins of all of us' (Is 53:6). He acted as a substitute in that he stood in our place, and so took upon himself the reality of our refusals, rejections and oppositions to the Father, whose Will he loved and did even now as he prepared to drink the chalice of suffering to the dregs. He carried our sins in his body all the way to the Cross (I P 2:21) out of love for the Father, and for us. The mercy that radiates from this action of his gives 'knowledge of a love that is beyond all knowledge' (Ep 3:18). 'Mercy', as Pope John Paul II writes, 'is love's second name'.[4]

The stunning originality of this should not be missed. All other religions seek a way out of, or beyond, the painful and negative dimensions of the human condition. They seek a relief from guilt, an escape from death, or a way into a region of bliss. This is understandable, since all religion addresses the human predicament. Jesus Christ however, went in the opposite direction. He lowered himself into our world, into our pain and forsakenness, into our death and sorrows, and though he is utterly beyond personal sin, he entered into solidarity with us to the point where 'he became sin for us' (II Co 5:21), as St Paul claims.

Our Blessed Saviour's experience of this dramatic encounter with sin is seen in his dying cry from the Cross, 'My God, My God, why have you forsaken me?' (Mk 15:34) In the act of sinning a person

18

forsakes God, and God, who has given us the supreme gift of personal freedom has to accept and ratify the sinner's desire. The sinner thus becomes God-forsaken. It is this forsakenness that the Redeemer entered into as 'he loved us to the end' (Jn 13:1). The combined weight of all these refusals was laid upon him.

On the summit of Calvary, however, he lost the effects of the beatifying vision. This was the torment of all torments. The summit of his loving us became the summit of his suffering. Both heaven and earth rejected him. Humanity crucified him and then he was forsaken. 'O all you who pass by look and see if there is any suffering like mine' (Lm 1:12).

Here God the Father manifests through his beloved Son, slain for sinners, a goodness so great that none greater can ever be thought of. The Pope's words are eloquent: 'The Cross of Christ is the most profound condescension of God to men, and to what humanity – especially in difficult and painful moments – looks on as its unhappy destiny. The Cross is like a touch of eternal love upon the most painful wounds of man's earthly existence; it is the total fulfilment of the messianic programme that Christ once formulated in the synagogue of Nazareth'.[5] This makes of Jesus Christ good news, inexhaustibly good news, for our generation.

Among the most painful wounds of today's society is a weakening of the religious sense. This shows itself in a lessening of faith and a cooling off of love. It also expresses itself as an emancipation from God which introduces practical agnosticism, even atheism, and a lifestyle which leaves God and the spiritual completely out of the picture. Where this happens, the meaning of life is lost. Furthermore, the great puzzles of human existence, such as the problem of evil, the struggle in the human heart between despair and hope, the conquest of spiritual sorrow, are left unanswered. Since these problems will not simply go away (because we remain human), people turn to alternatives such as humanly constructed religions and the many therapies and self-help groups which the psychoanalytic movement and psychology have made available. As human beings, we are a complexity of levels of body, psyche/mind and spirit. It is a fact of life that we experience breakdown of relationship at all these levels; and it is also true that we can experience the anxiety and guilt of the non-relatedness that follows. Sometimes this guilt can simply be morbid and neurotic, and the distinction between it and the guilt of a healthy conscience, while it may be clear in principle, is often confusing in practice. There are many reasons for this, but the most obvious one is that not many people reach a high level of moral maturity, and they carry within them from the past memories of moral training associated with fear and punishment. The guilt they suffer is a form of alienation from their true selves.

Psychotherapy, when wisely used, can restore in some way the fractured human psyche. But it can also have religious implications of immense proportions when it is open to the spiritual nature of persons and to the Christian truth that it is God who takes the initiative in any process that makes human beings pleasing to him. Divine therapy is pre-eminently a healing one. Christian revelation speaks of the divine presence as one of mercy, forgiveness and reconciliation: 'God was in Christ reconciling the world to himself, and not holding men responsible for their sins' (II Co 5:19). This means that sin – which in biblical terms means 'missing the mark' in our relationship to God – is a reality which afflicts the heart of human identity. Thus the search for that identity, the desire for meaning in life, is at heart the desire for divine forgiveness, forgiveness not only of moral guilt but of the existential guilt of our unholiness before the divine. God's forgiving love always, because it is God's, abounds even more than sin (see Rm 5:21) and human alienation. The Church exists in order to hand on this forgiveness of which each and every person has lasting need.

This is the context in which humanly constructed religions and merely human therapies emerge, are hopelessly inadequate because they are only human, and therefore not big enough to match the mystery and depth of human life. The human condition requires divine therapy. One might as well attempt to quarry granite with a razor, or moor a Cunard liner with a string, as to heal and save the human person with the small medicine of merely human techniques. Since the human person is created in 'the image and likeness of God' (Gn 1:27), only God can satisfy the ultimate aspirations of human life and liberate the soul from evil. That love 'will present us with a new and reconciled life' (Walter Kasper). The Church exists in order to hand on this forgiveness of which each and every person has lasting need.

A difficulty: 'We have no sin' (I Jn 1:10)
The message of God's forgiveness of sin is a central point in the New Testament and in the Creed. It always occurs in the third part of the Creed, is dependent on our belief in the Holy Spirit, and is associated with Baptism.[6] This message, however, is totally undermined by an attitude quite widespread today. It is the attitude 'which increasingly strives to free itself of any thought of guilt ... and which operates within a sinister framework of excuses'. This 'merciless attitude of modern society repeatedly encourages us to attempt to justify our acts and to suppress our guilt'.[7] In that way it cuts the ground from underneath the message of the forgiveness of sin.

The message of the forgiveness of sin encourages us to confess our sin: 'Father, I have sinned against heaven and against you' (Lk 15:18, 21). In this we see the truth that we are responsible for our actions; that our actions are either good or bad, and that they affect our relationship to God and his kingdom. We also note that God's eternal, merciful love, revealed in Christ, is continually available in the Church through the forgiveness of sins. This enables us to confess in the confidence of receiving forgiveness, healing and reconciliation.

Christian living and the forgiveness of sins
Christians, then, live their lives under the arc of the forgiving, merciful love of the Trinity, which 'lasts from age to age' (Lk 1:50). Citing those words, the Holy Father comments: 'We have every right to believe that our generation was included in the words of the Mother of God'.[8] The Church exists to communicate this divine mercy and forgiveness to people. Since this mercy is a primary attribute of God, indeed 'his second name', it is infinite, like him. 'No human sin can prevail over this power or even limit it. On the part of man only a lack of good will can limit it, a lack of readiness to be converted and to repent, in other words, persistence in obstinacy,

opposing grace and truth, especially in the face of the witness of the Cross and Resurrection of Christ'.[9]

To receive this mercy we must hear the gospel (see Rm 10:14-15). The message of Christ's merciful forgiveness creates a response of profound conversion in those who hear it. Conversion is always preceded by the discovery of this love that is 'patient and kind' (I Co 13:4) 'as only the Creator and Father can be'.[10] Christian living consists in large measure in keeping this love continually before us. We need to repent of our failures to accept it, and to celebrate God's mercy when we have sinned, and, finally, we try to have a heart full of mercy to those who sin against us. How could we receive God's mercy if we refuse this mercy to others? (see Mt 18:21-35).

It is no surprise, then, that at the centre of the Church's life there must be a 'pastoral practice of penance and reconciliation', which 'comprises all those tasks for which the Church is responsible on all levels in order to be able to promote both'.[11] Such practice flows from the Gospel as naturally as light from the sun or a stream from a powerful wellspring. Without this pastoral practice the Church's proclamation of the forgiveness of sins will be empty and fruitless. It would become, in the words of Dietrich Bonhoeffer, 'cheap grace', which 'amounts to a justification of sin and not of the sinner'. This is tantamount to 'preaching forgiveness without penance, baptism without communal discipline ..... and absolution without confession. Cheap grace is grace without anything succeeding it'.[12]

Personal and Communal Access to the Forgiving Christ

The Sacrament of Penance

After the gift of his Body for us, and his Blood shed for the remission of sins in the mystery of the Eucharist, the gift-sacrament of the forgiveness of sins is a most helpful and practical sacrament. What lies at the heart of this sacrament? Christ, the Good Shepherd, goes out to welcome and embrace the returning sinner with great joy, reinstates him in his Family-Body which the sinner has wounded and hurt by his sinning, and all this in the very moment the sinner 'comes to himself' and, moved by sorrow, turns to the Saviour with his baggage of sin (see Lk 15).

22

This happens through the mediation of the bishop or priest who represents Christ to the Church and the Church to Christ. This sacrament guarantees in this manner the personal access of Christ to the whole community. The new rites of reconciliation drawn up according to the directives of the Second Vatican Council are designed to bring out both the individual and communal dimensions of sin and forgiveness.

It is important to see in this sacrament the action of Christ our Head for the good of us, his members. This grace draws us towards him and away from sin. The sacrament is a call to conversion. It both presupposes conversion and advances conversion of heart and habits. In that way it powerfully helps us turn daily living into a holy journey to God. The sacrament brings about in the properly prepared a spiritual revolution of mind, the decision not to be conformed to the world (see Rm 12:2) but rather to the standards of Christ and his kingdom. This conversion-perspective on the sacrament, though central in earlier centuries, was inadequately grasped during recent centuries. The Church now reminds us of it.

NOTES

1.   *Nostra Aetate* 1
2.   *GS* 9
3.   *GS* 10
4.   *DM* 7
5.   *DM* 8
6.   See J.N.D. Kelly, *Early Christian Creeds*, 5th edition, London, 1977, *passim.*
7.   W. Kasper, 'The Church and the Forgiveness of Sins', in *Communio* 2(1989), 163.
8.   *DM* 10
9.   *DM* 13
10. *DM* 13
11. Synod of Bishops, *Reconciliatio et Paenitentia* (1984), 23.
12. D. Bonhoeffer, *The Cost of Discipleship*, London, 1959, 36.

3

THE CONTEMPORARY SCENE: DESCRIPTION AND ANALYSIS OF THE NEW AGE

Since the 1960s western civilisation has experienced great unrest. Combined with progress in the fields of science and technology, great material wealth on the personal front, and unparalleled exploration of space, there is deep personal and social unease. The modern person is often unhappy. None of our achievements have produced what we most need, peace of mind, and peace among nations, combined with justice for the individual and society. The modern utopia has produced family and social disintegration on a vast scale. Modern means of communication have had the effect of isolating the individual, who feels lost in a world that has become a global village.

Secular humanism, atheistic materialism, rationalism and religious scepticism, which were so popular in the early part of this century, left a great void in the human heart. Unfortunately, our secular society did not look to God to fill this void. Instead, it turned to eastern religions in search of a new mysticism. The result was a flood of gurus who came to teach the west how to meditate. They introduced yoga, transcendental meditation, mantras and related teachings, but without reference to Christ, the Church, or revealed truth. Many Christians have participated in these exercises, even thinking they could 'Christianise' them by using Christian language to explain what is essentially non-Christian, for example the use of so-called 'Christian' mantras, and putting Christian explanations on yoga or TM practices. But these gurus taught the only thing they knew, which is Hinduism, and the Hindu Pantheon.

This movement coincided with a new interest in psychology, not as a science, but as a tool to help solve personal problems.[1] Thus, encounter groups and self-help groups became very popular. The tendency has been to turn away from the teaching of the Church

24

to this new psychology to find answers to life's problems, and to overcome the sense of powerlessness experienced by many in today's world. To a considerable extent the Church's moral teaching has been put to one side, while people seek secular answers to life.

The problems of the past thirty years have seen the Peace Movement, the Environmental Movement, the Holistic Health Movement, the Human Potential Movement, the Women's Movement and many other movements arise in response to the problems that confront the 'global village'. Included among them is the New Age Movement (which will be referred to by the abbreviation NAM), which is the subject of this document.

Roots of the New Age Movement

The New Age has divergent roots. It is a modern revival of pagan religions with a mixture of influences from both eastern religions and also from modern psychology, philosophy, science,[2] and the counterculture that developed in the 1950s and 1960s.[3] Zen Buddhism has had great influence, with its emphasis on the higher consciousness, or the true self, and seeking enlightenment.[4] Hinduism is another major influence, and a combination of them is seen in the emphasis on reincarnation, the stress on Karma, and the need for meditation to find one's Higher Self.[5]

The NAM claims that we have moved into a new astrological age, the Age of Aquarius, and that the human race has made a paradigm shift in its thinking. It says that we have moved from 'left brain' rational thinking to 'right brain' intuitive thinking. Therefore we are the age of 'the spirit', the age of the 'new mysticism'.[6] Marilyn Ferguson says 'that after a dark, violent age, the Piscean, we are entering a millenium of love and light ... the time of "the mind's true liberation".'[7]

Although called 'New Age', this movement is not new. Its roots go back to the very first major attack on Christianity in the first century. At that time it was called Gnosticism, and the early Church Fathers fought it vigorously. 'Gnostic influence on New Age thought is unmistakable, as new Age leaders freely acknowledge'.[8] Like its modern counterpart Gnosticism was an eclectic,

25

hybrid movement,[9] which borrowed elements from eastern religions, Judaism, Christianity, and the philosophies of the time. Only the initiated few who have the secret knowledge or wisdom (the gnosis), know that humans are 'divine', and must struggle to regain their divinity by a journey into forbidden territory, as far as the Church is concerned.[10]

Another major root of the NAM is the the Transcendental Movement. These teachers borrowed from the holy books of the eastern religions, and adapted the material to suit the western mind which was materialistic, and this-world centred. So, transcendental meditation was presented, not as a religious exercise involving initiation into Hinduism, but as an exercise for relaxation! Yoga travelled a similar path. It was presented as a merely physical exercises to relax the body, and enhance health. Because of the western presentation of these eastern spiritual exercises, vast numbers of Christians have involved themselves in them, some claiming to have 'christianised' them.

Marilyn Ferguson admits that the transcendentalists and Masonry were important antecedents to the NAM.[11] William Thompson discusses the occult background of the NAM in the paper entitled 'Sixteen Years into the New Age', published in *Reimagination of the World* by David Spangler/ William Thompson. He admits that Freemasonary is an important vehicle for the transmission of these ideas.[12] Benjamin Creme says that the new religion that will emerge from the NAM 'will manifest through organisations like the Masonry. In Freemasonry is embedded the core or the secret heart of the occult mysteries ...' He goes on to say that it is 'through the Orders of Masonry that the Initiatory Path will be trodden ... and also through the purified churches' (purified by the NAM teachings, that is).[13]

A deeply successful root of the New Age is the Spiritualist Movement, which became popular in the nineteenth century. This was the origin of Theosophy, the creation of Helena Blavatsky (1831-91), whose writings have deeply influenced NAM thinking.[14] Two of her successors, Annie Besant and Guy Ballard, continued her work, and are influential in their writings.[15] William Thompson admits that the New Age is not new but he calls it 'the planetisation of the esoteric'.[16] Elliot Miller adds that 'occultism, as represented by the NAM, is rapidly becoming a force to be reckoned with in the western world.'[17]

Rejection of Christianity

The leaders and writers of the NAM claim that Christianity has failed. To them it is obsolete. It represents the 'old age thinking', the Piscean Age that has passed, so it should be either transformed by NAM teaching or 'dealt with', a point we shall look at later. First, NAM tries to transform it, just as it tries to transform the political and social structures of society.[18] That transformation lies in mixing Christianity with eastern religions initially, then with the occult. William Thompson says that 'Christianity needs Buddhism. Paradoxically, Buddhism plays Redeemer to Christianity, just as Christianity played Redeemer to Judaism'.[19] Elsewhere the same author says 'that what Christianity was to Judaism, science is to Christianity. Science is to reform Christianity...'.[20]

Other NAM writers speak in the same vein: Benjamin Creme asserts that ' the Churches have gone very far away from the religion which the Christ inaugurated ...'.[21] The 'old age theology' of the Church is now put aside,[22] because 'religion is more often than not reactionary: it sees the sacred as the previous level of evolution; it sees the emergent as the profane ... 'Religion', he says, 'is sacerdotal and not sacred; it is a too-restrictive celebration of the previous level of evolution'. He admits that the fundamentalists are right in viewing the NAM as irreligious *on their terms*.[23]

Religion is not condemned *per se*, however, for it is useful. 'It can be sweet and loving and administer to the victims of earthquakes ... but is too passive, too reactive, to be creative enough to imagine a novel emergence ... the sacerdotal is all tied up in and with the past'.[24] They blame the Christian Church for putting guilt on everyone because it teaches that we must repent of our sins in order to be saved. They claim that there is no sin, and that salvation is self-made. According to them, problems can be solved through psychology, eastern religions, the occult, or any combination of them.[25] In her chapter called 'Introductory Remarks', Alice Bailey lists the churches and religions under the heading of 'negative groups' which must be dealt with,[26] because 'religion as a whole has gone astray ... because the eyes of the theologians have been on the material, phenomenal aspect of life, through fear ....'.[27] The entity D.K., dictating this text, is quite sure that both Christianity and Judaism must be eliminated in their present form. Speaking about the new festivals that are emerging through NAM, it says that 'the Christian Church has so distorted its mission and ruthlessly perverted the intention for which He (The NAM 'Christ' manifesting through the Disciple Jesus) originally manifested...' that it is not very useful in its present form.[28] 'The failure of Christianity can be traced to its Jewish background ...' claims this spirit who 'has already pointed out the faults in world religions and their obsolete theologies ... and also the evils of Judaism'.[29] Some of these faults are 'the political scheming of the Vatican, its exploitation of the masses, and its emphasis on ignorance ...,[30] and their ridiculous belief that they know what is in the Mind of God ...'.[31] The ignorance referred to here is the fact that most Christians are not mystics, or do not claim mystical experience. They are seen as adhering to the externals of religion without knowing its inner content.

In a discussion paper on 'The Bringing Forth of Worlds', William Thompson goes further, and speaks about the role of evil in the New Age and in the Church. He says that 'the real dynamic of the New Age is happening where nobody is looking – namely, in just those profane areas ... warfare, pollution, and the light and shadow economies of the globe. In other words, the revelation is taking place at the edges of our peripheral vision in such ignored areas as "noise" and "evil" (quotation marks his).'[32] Since, according to him, 'there is no single Messiah, then there is no single hierarchy with God the Father and the pope at the top and humanity at the bottom' (ibid.). Therefore, he asserts that 'we need the Other to rescue us' from Christianity,[33] and the context would appear to locate this 'Other' in evil!

Initially he says that this encounter with the 'Other' can be Buddhism, it can be angels ... dolphins ...or extra-terrestrials as one learns to expand one's consciousness (ibid.). He says that religion generates evil: 'the vision of complexity in the energising of evil is there for all to see in the gospel of John, for Judas cannot betray Jesus until he is given a sop of vinegar. In other words, a negative – a shadow – Eucharist empowers Judas, just as the others are empowered by bread and wine' (ibid.). 'If one unconsciously ignores the role of evil in Christianity ... one ends up playing it out in the cruelty and passionate hatreds that are so characteristic of those committed to a doctrinal view of life. The fanatically devout generate the Other in the kinds of religious warfare we see today in Northern Ireland and Beirut .... One of the greatest forces for evil in the world today, is religion'.[34] Creme says that 'it has been the tremendous triumph of the forces of evil that the churches throughout the centuries have been allowed to monopolise the idea of spirituality: what is to do with the church and religion is spiritual and everything else is not'.[35]

Ascended Masters of Wisdom: New Age Religion
The NAM sees God, not as a personal being, but an impersonal force that can be manipulated. Their thinking does not appear to be altogether clear, even though they use terms such as ' Force, Energy, Essence, Consciousness, Vibration, Principle and Being' to describe God. Their idea seems to be that 'It' is infinite but impersonal.[36] When asked 'What do you mean by God?', Creme replied that 'It' should be spoken of 'in planetary terms, because this planet is actually a vehicle of expression for a Cosmic Entity, a great Heavenly Man. It is a Centre in the body of God of our solar system .... The planetary Logos is a little God in a bigger God which is the systemic Logos – which Itself is only a little God in an even bigger galactic system – at the centre of which is another greater God.' Then he goes on to speak of a hierarchy of beings that is somehow part of this system. 'There is a gradation of divinity from the lowest crystal of the mineral world up to and beyond the Galactic God himself, about Whom we can say nothing at all. This is not a man but a Great Consciousness'.[37]

NAM believes that there are other beings in the universe whom they call 'Ascended Masters'. These are said to be especially evolved beings, who can be either the dead, or spirits. Spangler says of them: 'These formative forces (which are at work in those

29

who open up to Cosmic Consciousness in meditation) ... are mediated and directed by purposeful entities whom we might call angels or archangels, along with other beings both human and non-human who work out the specific application and incarnation of these forces'.[38] Meditators allow themselves to be guided by these entities through a process called channelling, which involves becoming a medium, whereby they permit themselves to be taken over by these spirits and guided by them.

Alice Bailey speaks about a special group of Ascended Masters called 'The Hierarchy' who appear to be very much involved in the affairs of humanity through those who open up to Cosmic Consciousness. These are especially evolved beings who guide people who seek spiritual help through the channelling process. She describes them as 'human beings who have lived, suffered, achieved, failed, attained success, endured death and passed through the experience of resurrection. They are the same in nature as are those who struggle today' on earth. All states of consciousness are known to them and they have mastered them all ... their great Master is the Christ (who is not a person according to them).[39]

Some of these Masters have become internationally known, such as the famous 'Ramtha' who is channelled by Mrs J.Z. Knight, who holds public seminars to allow the spirit to teach and guide others. There is also Lazaris, who is channelled by Jack Pursell, and a host of others, many of which masquerade under biblical names to confuse people. Two entities calling themselves 'Christ' , and 'John' are channelled by David Spangler, one of the world leaders of the NAM. He has written a book under this influence called *Revelations on the Christ*.[40] Since channelling involves both the personality of the medium and that of the entity, there must be signs of two sources at work, one human, the other preternatural, i.e. from a source outside nature, that is not God. (This is usually called the supernatural in the NAM). Randall N. Baer, a former top New Age leader and writer in America says that channelling is the single most influential phenomenon inside the New Age today.[41] It became popular in the 1980s when everyone had to be taught by these 'ascended masters', which are variously called 'The Council of the Twelve' for the properly initiated, or simply extra-terrestrials, dolphins, or spirit-gods to others.[42] Russell Chandler claims that the NAM is a descent into darkness, one which occurs subtly, almost imperceptively, as the helpful gives way to the dubious, and the dubious descends to the dangerous.[43] The NAM claims that these ascended masters can teach wisdom and bring us to true enlightenment.[44] Yet former NAM devotees like Elliot Miller and Randall Baer testify that they were led into spirit infestation that they do not hesitate to call demonic.[45]

Trance channelling: NAM spiritual experience

The trance channelling process involves the medium's personality being taken over by this other entity, so that the medium is 'absent' in some way. During the channelling the medium has no control over her body or any of her faculties. Both body and mind are operated by the spirit, who speaks, 'walks around' etc. through this person. During the seminar the spirit appears to use mass hypnosis on the audience while it teaches its doctrines, works miracles, and promises to work others.[46] Baer confirms that the revelations given through trance channelling come from the spirit world, but not from God. The source is the occult, but cloaked in words of love and light in order to deceive.[47]

The type of teachings given by these spirit entities are: 'You are your own saviour'; 'there is no death'; 'love yourself and be happy' and 'You are god. Create your own reality'.[48] Their teachings are consistently occultic and anti-biblical.[49] The altered states of consciousness required for this trance channelling are usually induced by specific techniques, rituals, drugs and other volitional efforts of those involved.[50] Baer describes the NAM as Satan's web of 'luminous darkness'.[51] He claims that millions of people are allowing their lives to be guided directly or indirectly by these spirits through books dictated by them, or tape recordings of their sessions.

Helena Blavatsky warns her readers that 'one of the Seven Accursed Sciences – or the Seven Arts of enchantment of the Gnostics ... is now before the public, pregnant with danger in the present as for the future. The modern name for it is hypnotism. In the ignorance of the seven principles (used by occultists), and used by scientific and ignorant materialists, it will soon become Satanism in the full acceptation of the term' (capitals hers).[52] Here we have the greatest teacher of NAM pointing out the danger of using the technique of hypnotism, yet it is used widely and is considered to be harmless by society today.

Familiar Spirits: NAM Spiritual Guidance

Trance channelling is not the only spirit activity popular in the NAM. There are various methods of acquiring familiar spirits, disguised as 'counsellors', or friends to advise people in their decision-making. They can be acquired through mind control techniques that use counsellors in the so-called 'laboratory' of the heart in a step-by-step relaxation of mind and body technique that is offered by some groups, such as the Silva Mind Control, as a non-religious way of making oneself more productive in learning, mental work, or more successful in business. This practice is used in self-help groups for healing, relaxation, and creativity enhancement.

These counsellors can be anybody, including the dead or demonic spirits. From the time these spirits are engaged, one is told to pray to them and ask their advice on everything. This opens the soul to demonic influence as we have no control over the forces involved, because the person has been put into a relaxed state in which they are ready to receive any influence without using the filter of intelligence or rational thinking. The process also makes the faculty of the will supple and compliant, and ready to receive any stimulus. This is a basic NAM technique for developing higher states of consciousness. 'This practice of engaging familiar spirits is one of the most diverse, pervasive, and influential NAM methods in use today'.[53] Texe Marrs claims that the Silva Mind Control practice is based on occult philosophy, simply repackaged in de-religionised form for the materialistic west.[54] Silva Mind Control teaches that the subconscious mind can be programmed to achieve any desired goal.[55]

David Spangler claims that there is a higher form of communication with these spirits than channelling. In his book *Revelation:*

The Birth of a New Age he says that meditation opens a person up to a new level of consciousness. If this individual joins a group *at this level* he or she can learn to let go of individual consciousness and develop group consciousness. The individual with aptitude can then learn either separately or in the group to allow 'another consciousness' from 'another level' to 'manifest' through them by 'fusing' with this being.[56] Thus an entity calling itself 'John' manifests through Spangler. Spangler claims that this 'fusing': 'I am you and you are I',[57] is superior to channelling, because he and 'John' are ONE, so that John speaks through Spangler.[58] Thus, Spangler claims to be a mystic.

The Findhorn community manifested other entities through the group,[59] because they developed this group consciousness (or entered into group initiation). Thus the entity calling itself 'Limitless love and truth' manifested itself by giving 'revelation' through the most sensitive one, namely Spangler. The transmissions of this entity form the major part of *Revelation: The Birth of a New Age*, from chapter 4 onwards. Sometimes this spirit speaks as if it were 'god', sometimes it admits that it is separate from God.[60] Yet it claims to be the source of a 'new heaven and a new earth' (ibid.). After they were asked to 'live the life of this presence',[61] the group saw itself as 'a centre for materialisation' of this entity.[62] The entity needed the group in order to manifest.[63] It identifies itself as: 'I am the Light' (ibid.). The transmissions of this entity form part of the 'new scriptures' of the NAM, hence the title of the book. All other serious leaders claim to have 'messages' from spirit entities, for example Creme gets his from Lord Maitreya.[64]

The Lucifer connection: The NAM 'Light' experience
Both the old Gnosticism and the present NAM use the occult to achieve their so-called 'new' spirituality. They proclaim that we are in a new age of the spirit, but the spirits they follow are dangerous and misleading. Marrs says that the NAM believes that the sun is a divine, living being, called the Solar Father. Lucifer is claimed to be the Solar Logos (Word), a god spirit appointed by the Solar Father to usher in the New Age through the Luciferic initiation of humanity.[65]

Spangler says that 'Lucifer comes to give us the final .. Luciferic initiation .. it is the initiation into the New Age'. He also says that 'Christ is the same force as Lucifer ... Lucifer prepares man for the experience of christhood .... Lucifer works within each one of us to bring us to wholeness as we move into the New Age'.[66] Spangler teaches that Lucifer is 'an agent of God's love'.[67] He believes that Lucifer is the angel of man's inner evolution, that 'the light that reveals to us the path to Christ comes from Lucifer...the great initiator.....Lucifer comes to give us the final initiation....that many people in the days ahead will be facing, for it is an initiation into the New Age' (ibid.).

Spangler is not alone in this teaching, however. Eklal Kueshana, a leader of a mystical group calling itself 'The Stelle Group' published a book called *The Ultimate Frontier* twenty-five years ago, revealing that Lucifer is the Head of the secret Brotherhood of spirits, the highest order one can reach in the spiritual quest. In his book he claims that up to recently only a privileged few had been accepted into this enlightened brotherhood, but that now it was open to those brave enough to walk the spiritual path. This initiation is an entrance into the Great White Brotherhood, also known variously as the great White Lodge, the Masters of Wisdom, the Hierarchy of angels around the throne.[68]

In NAM circles Lucifer is also referred to under the titles of Sant, Nat, Tanat, Sat Guru, and Sanat.[69] The Lucis Foundation and the Association for Research and Development in Virginia, which appears to be the brain centre for the NAM, defends the use of the term 'Lucifer' as meaning the 'light-bringer' and the 'morning star' in order to throw off the charge of Satanism.[70]

Spangler also refutes the charge of Satanism saying that he 'was careful to distinguish between Satan, a term he used for the presence of evil in the world, and Lucifer'.[71] Yet, William Thompson, who co-authors this book, says that 'Lucifer and Christ are the twin sides of the demiurgic power of the manifest universe, just as Judas and John are the light and shadow sides of the historic world of Christendom'.[72]

Creme, in his book *The Reappearance of Christ and the Masters of Wisdom*, says that the aspect of God that we aspire to is the

34

Logos of our planet, who is embodied for us as Sanat Kumara, on Shamballa. He is our 'Father'. ...In the coming age many, many people will see God as Sanat Kumara and take the third initiation .... When you take the third initiation you see God, as Sanat Kumara, the Lord of the world, who is a real physical being in etheric matter on Shamballa'.[73]

Creme also claims that Lord Maitreya, the NAM Christ, is the underling of the great Sanat. Once a person has been initiated by Christ Maitreya (the first and second initiations) they become eligible for the third initiation by 'God' Sanat. This third initiation is the important Luciferic initiation. Creme also refers to Sanat as 'The Ancient of Days' the term applied by the Old Testament to God the Father.[74] Alice Bailey identifies Lucifer as 'the ruler of humanity', the 'son of the morning' and 'the prodigal son'.[75]

The source of the NAM teachings is Helena Blavatsky's two-volume work *The Secret Doctrine*. In *Anthropogenesis* (volume two), from pp. 506-518, she deals with the question of the identity of this Lucifer to which the NAM teachers refer. Is this entity what Christians call Satan? She says that 'the "Old Dragon" or "Satan" ... is that Angel who was proud enough to believe himself God; brave enough to buy his independence at the price of eternal suffering and torture; beautiful enough to have adored himself in full divine light; strong enough to reign in darkness amidst agony, and to have built himself a throne on his inextinguishable pyre.' Here she was quoting a famous cabbalist called Eliphas Levi, and she says that the definition is correct. But she adds that 'this devil is mankind'![76] This has to be so for we are 'god' and this god is the source of good and evil. Both God and Satan are found within us.

Yet, like the NAM teachers who follow her, she then discusses both God and Satan as separate from us. Referring to God she says that the Jewish God, Jehovah, was 'one of the subordinate Spirits at best, that this Spirit is "the Spirit of the Earth".'[77] It would seem that Lucifer belongs to a higher level of reality than this! She quotes the cabbalists as saying that 'the true name of Satan is that of Jehovah upside down, for 'Satan is not a black god but the negation of a white deity'. He is *the light of truth*. 'The Devil is not a person but a creative Force, for Good as for Evil'.[78]

35

Later she shows that Lucifer *is* that Light that these initiates are seeking: 'the great magic agent ... astral light ... is that which the Church calls Lucifer.' She acknowledges that the Latin scholastics called this entity Satan.[79] Quoting Levi again she refers to Lucifer as 'the Astral Light ... which serves to create and destroy. ... This Light therefore, inasmuch as it is devouring, revengeful, and fatal would thus really be hell-fire, the serpent of the legend; the tormented errors of which it is full, the tears and gnashing of teeth of the abortive beings it devours, the phanthom of life that escapes them, and seems to mock and insult their agony, all this would be the devil or Satan indeed' (ibid.).

According to Blavatsky this Astral Light 'is the universal Soul, the Matrix of the Universe, the Mysterium Magnum, which, with regard to humankind, manifests itself by the effects it produces in persons and nations. She says that 'Lucifer is the name of the Angelic Entity presiding over *the light of truth* (italics hers) as over the light of day ... so, to the profane the Astral Light may be God and Devil at once.'[80] Lucifer is divine and terrestrial light, the 'Holy Ghost' and 'Satan' (quotation marks hers) at one and the same time....[81] As he was responsible for the Fall, in which the eyes of the human race were opened, he is therefore the source of Wisdom and Knowledge (ibid.). 'And now it stands proven', she says, 'that Satan, or the Red *Firey* Dragon, the "Lord of Phosphorus" and Lucifer, or "Light Bearer" ' are one and the same reality. She claims that 'it' exists within us (ibid.). Finally, when discussing the 'Verbum' or the 'Son' she states that 'the Verbum and Lucifer are one in their dual aspect' (ibid.).

One can see therefore, that later writers of the NAM have picked up these ideas and know what they are doing in 'seeking the light', and attributing Wisdom to Lucifer. Those who follow the path of Lucifer are called 'light bearers' in the world.[82] John Price calls upon his followers to join this gathering of 'light bearers' to form the 'critical mass'[83] of humanity needed to change the world forever. He calls them the 'new wayshowers' for modern society. In this context St Paul's warning in II Corinthians 11:14 about Satan disguising himself as an angel of light makes a lot of sense.

Initiations: The path towards the light

The Initiatory Path is one of the sure ways to enlightenment. Without initiations one is seen to dabble in these ideas, but not seriously.[84] Baer claims that these initiations involve a ritual infusion of occult mystical power into the recipient 'who thereby receives various gifts, powers, and awakenings'.[85] Baer claims that one experiences powerful altered states of consciousness involving bliss, joy and love that hook the initiated into the experience. Each initiation is seen as a major spiritual breakthrough into new plateaux of higher consciousness and psychic powers (ibid.).

Creme explains that 'the esoteric process known as Initiation is the scientific path to this perfectionment, whereby man becomes united and at-one with his Source. This path of perfectionment is marked off by five major steps or points of crisis and tension. Each initiation results in a tremendous expansion of awareness or consciousness which brings an ever deepening and more inclusive vision and knowledge of the true nature of reality. No Master of the fifth Initiation needs any further incarnational experience on Earth' because at this point he has completed his Karmic cycle.[86]

Alice Bailey, in her major work *The Rays and Initiations*, says that the time for individual initiation is over.[87] What is required now is group initiation. Her book gives detailed instruction on how to achieve this. She claims that the contents of her book were dictated by the entity identified as D.K., otherwise known as Master Djwhal Khul, the Tibetan, an ascended master. It was published in 1960 in time for the universalisation of the occult through the NAM.

The Christ connection: The NAM Messiah

Lord Maitreya is the name given to the expected New Age Messiah announced by Benjamin Creme, who appears to be his prophet.[88] This 'messiah' has nothing to do with the Second Coming of Jesus in glory, but the language used by the NAM leaders is confusing, as they use Christian terms to get across their own occult teachings. Creme publicly proclaimed in 1976 that Maitreya was manifesting himself on the higher planes of consciousness first, and only when the time was ripe would he manifest materially. In the meantime he is transmitting messages through Creme and his group.[89]

Who *is* this coming New Age Messiah? Creme says that 'all the great religions hold before humanity the idea of a further revelation which will be given by a future Teacher or Avatar. Christians hope for Christ's return, the Buddhists look for the coming of another Buddha, the Lord Maitreya, while the Muslims await the coming of the Imam Mahdi, the Hindus, the Bodhisattva or Krishna, and the Jews the Messiah. Each of them expects a Coming One, a Revealer of new truths and a Guide into the future. Esotericists know them all as one Being, the World Teacher, the supreme Head of the Spiritual Hierarchy of Masters, and look for his imminent return now as we enter the Aquarian Age'.[90] Creme explains later that this 'Christ is an agent. The Christ is not God. When I say, "the coming of Christ", I don't mean the coming of God'.[91] On the subject of the Return of Christ Alice Bailey states that there is a growing belief 'that the Christ *is* in us, as He was in the Master Jesus, and this belief will alter world affairs and mankind's entire attitude to life'.[92] Jesus of Nazareth is 'the Master Jesus' who was 'Christed' during his lifetime – just as we are! He is just an ordinary human being who needed to work through his own karmic cycle in endless incarnations. Since Creme claims to be 'overshadowed' by the Returning Christ, he is on the same level as 'the Master Jesus.' Bailey points out that Jesus will not be returning to the Earth. Neither will The Christ for that matter, for 'he cannot return because he has always been here upon the Earth watching over the destiny of humanity.' He can only reappear.[93]

This coming NAM 'Christ' is also called 'The Cosmic Christ', who will be manifested to and in people worldwide. In a discussion paper on the subject Spangler and Thompson admit that they are speaking in a Buddhist cosmology, and that it is not necessary to keep 'all this composting heap of Christianity' to explain their ideas.[94] They relegate the story of Jesus of Nazareth to myth, specifically the myth of the sacred child who saves us.[95] Spangler and other NAM writers dismiss Jesus as having no good authority for today. He is merely one of the more enlightened ones.[96]

Spangler explains the nature of this Cosmic Christ as 'the essence of all evolving life; he lives within all. From the Christ Life of the Logos down to the Christ Life of the simplest pebble or organism, he was present in the foundations of the Earth.' He says that there is 'Christ potential' in everything, 'the Christ energies' that call us forth in evolution. Like all other NAM teachers he claims that the Buddha, the Enlightened or Awakened One, was the first to embody the Christ, and radiate its energy to the Earth. The Buddha led humanity forward until Jesus of Nazareth, who was the next to embody the Christ energies for the human race. We are now expecting a third individual to do the same ... the new messiah that NAM is expecting will materialise soon.[97]

Creme says that in the esoteric tradition 'the Christ is not the name of an individual but of an Office in the Hierarchy. The present holder of the office, the Lord Maitreya, has held it for 2,600 years, and manifested in Palestine through his Disciple, Jesus, by the occult method of overshadowing ...'.[98] He further states that the Masters of the Hierarchy are now ready to return. They will come with Maitreya, and will 'walk openly among us ... and their presence in the world will be an established fact' (ibid.). One of the reasons for their coming is that their own evolutionary development demands it! They must emerge as a group and demonstrate how they can function simultaneously on all planes of reality .... then presumably we, humans, will follow suit![99]

The Church is wrong, Creme says, in attributing some absolute form of divinity to Jesus.[100] 'Jesus *is* divine but in the way that you and I are divine." He goes on to say that Jesus is an evolving being just like everybody else (ibid.). He is 'not the one and only Son of God, but the friend and Elder Brother of Humanity' (ibid.). Creme explains Jesus as a fifth stage Initiate, hence a Master, and illustrates this with a reinterpretation of Gospel passages.[101] He says that Jesus 'was, and still is, a Disciple of the Christ ... By the occult process of overshadowing, the Christ, Maitreya, took over and worked through the body of Jesus from the Baptism onwards'.[102] Hence one must not look for the biblical Christ in this new event.[103]

In answering the question: 'What happened the consciousness of Jesus when he was overshadowed by the Christ?' Creme said that 'the body was that of Jesus. From the Baptism onwards, sometimes Jesus himself was in it; sometimes Jesus *and* the Christ used it

39

simultaneously; while at still other times the Christ alone manifested through it. The consciousness of Jesus became the observer of all that took place'.[104] This not only explains why they separate Jesus from 'The Christ' but also explains Creme's own assertion that he, too, is overshadowed by this 'Christ'! His description of it demands possession or oneness of some kind.[105]

The Great Invocation: NAM official prayer

From the point of Light
within the Mind of God
Let Light stream forth into
the minds of men.
Let Light descend to the Earth.

From the point of Love
within the Heart of God
Let Love stream forth into
the hearts of men.
May Christ return to the Earth.

From the centre where the
Will of God is known
Let purpose guide the little
wills of men –
The purpose which the
Masters know and serve.

From the centre which we
call the race of men
Let the Plan of Love and
Light work out.
And may it seal the door
where evil dwells.

Let Light and Love and
Power restore the Plan
on Earth

The 'Great Invocation', the NAM 'official prayer', is used to call upon the New Age 'Christ' to come now. NAM defends itself from the religious charge by saying that it is merely calling on the collective unconscious of the universe to bring on the New Age. They believe that if 'a critical mass' of people throughout the world join in this invocation the massive energy generated by this would bring on the Christ.[106] The occult leader, Alice Bailey, is the source of the Great Invocation, which is explained in great detail in her book *The Externalisation of the Hierarchy* in which she reveals The Plan of the Hierarchy of Beings for this planet Earth. Because the Invocation is couched in 'love and light' language, many Christians are using it, not realising that they are invoking these entities.

Creme gives instructions to his followers on how to use this prayer effectively: They mentally visualise the Buddha at stanza one, then the sun representing the Light coming to Earth, while remembering that the phrase 'may Christ return to the Earth' refers to the Hierarchy. There is more power released if they pray in groups.[107] Constance Cumbey, in *The Hidden Dangers of the Rainbow*, shows that there has been a worldwide distribution of the Great Invocation by World Goodwill, and that it has been accepted by people of every culture and religion. This prayer can be interpreted in the light of its makers and users.[108]

New Age spirituality: Discovering our own divinity

The so-called 'spirituality' of the NAM could be called 'spiritual humanism'. The corner-stone of this humanism is the belief that humankind is divine in nature, and is therefore, essentially 'god', or an enlightened god-man.[109] Whereas secular humanism denies deity, and exalts our own intellectual, creative, moral powers as the way to find true meaning to life, spiritual humanism affirms deity, one that casts us in the role of a higher race of cosmic gods. This spiritual humanism is born of a deep-seated disillusionment with much of the mainstream western values and institutions, especially the Church. It was born of an intense search for an alternative way of solving life's biggest problems.[110]

Marilyn Ferguson, whose book *The Aquarian Conspiracy*

41

brought the NAM to the masses, says that God is the sum total of consciousness in the universe expanding through human evolution. She proclaims that the radical centre of the spiritual experience is 'knowing without doctrine'.[111] She further claims that those who persevere with this 'transformative process' give up conventional Christianity and Christian dogma.[112] The gurus, she explains, merely teach techniques, but they positively discourage religious dogma as second-hand knowledge. The seeker must learn by personal experience. This so-called mystical journey leads to the 'white light experience'.[113]

Miller confirms that personal experience is the all important factor for the NAM. He says that 'for the responsive subject, "ASCs" (altered states of consciousness) can produce a profound mystical sense of "transcendence" of individuality and identification with everything. Such experiences of undifferentiated consciousness suggest to the seeker that ultimate reality itself is undifferentiated; everything is one, and the nature of the One must be consciousness'.[114] He further states that the person who passively submits to, or pursues ASCs, 'is setting himself up for a religious conversion' (ibid.), that may be either a 'passageway to reality, or a passageway to delusion.'[115]

One of the problems is that the mystical states that ensue have such an impact on the psyche that the person becomes *absolutely certain* of what they experience. These people tend to think that they alone *understand reality* and consider Christians who have to believe without seeing (cf. Jn 20:28) as unenlightened souls. Because of their absolute certainty it is very difficult for rational arguments to penetrate their thinking. Their response is that you 'do not know'. The people who are most vulnerable to this experience are the humanists or materialists who are experiencing the spiritual as real for the first time (ibid.).

Counterfeit religion

We live in the age of the counterfeit. It is so acceptable to have a copy of an original that we hardly think about it. Women wear counterfeit jewels that look just as good as the real thing. The paper copy of the master painting looks good. The wood veneer

42

looks as good as real wood. The plastic version of an object is commonplace. Today, counterfeit religion is also available, and it, too, looks superficially like the real thing. The NAM is a religious system even though its leaders cloak it with humanistic or pseudo-scientific language. It is religious syncretism, a mixture of the occult with aspects of eastern mysticism, neopaganism and human potential psychology.[116] NAM speakers say that 'All religions are essentially the same', especially at the deeper levels, so there is no room for a religion like Judaism or Christianity that is based in a historical revelation that does not change (ibid.). To them revelation is continuous, and they are the new bearers of the word, and consequently the new leaders of humanity.[117]

Marilyn Ferguson admits that the NAM looks for a personal religion, but outside the mainstream of Christianity.[118] She says that among the millions now engaged in the New Age search, many, if not most, were drawn into it almost unawares. They were already moving away from the Christian Churches and from Judaism towards eastern religions. It was a shift from a religion mediated by authority to one of personal experience. 'Now the heretics are gaining ground' she says. 'Doctrine is losing its authority, and knowing is superseding belief'.[119]

Many in the NAM pride themselves on being tolerant of all spiritual paths, because they say that all paths lead to the same place. But when confronted with biblical Christianity they are hostile, accusing Christians of being judgmental, and rigidly dogmatic. They do not accept the notion of Christian revealed truth, while accepting all that they receive through their spirit entities, and out-of-the-body experiences.[120] It is objective truth that they reject, while accepting subjective experience, apparently without discernment. A whole new series of Bible commentaries has been published by the New Age Bible and Philosophy Centre in Santa Monica, California. These books, called *New Age Bible Interpretation*, are an all-out assault on the Bible.[121] Examples of reinterpretation of the gospels are found in all references to Jesus of Nazareth in these NAM writings. Reinterpretation of The Fall, Redemption, Grace all abound in these books. Helena Blavatsky, for example, speaks of 'the metaphorical Fall, just as we have the metaphorical atonement and crucifixion .... and the God-slandering doctrine of Hell...'.[122]

Counterfeit doctrine

The NAM teaches the doctrine of reincarnation, which is a teaching of Hinduism. This denies that we meet God in death in order to face his particular Judgment which decides whether we are ready for Heaven, or unworthy of his presence, either temporarily or permanently. Instead they say that we are recycled back to the earth in an endless number of lives until we reach perfection by our own efforts. It is because of this belief that death ceases to have meaning, so the NAM justifies the killing of infants in abortion, also suicide and euthanasia. After all, these souls are merely sent on to a higher state to reconsider their position and return in a body they are prepared to work with until they reach perfection by completing their karma!

The law of karma means that we incur spiritual debt throughout our lifetime which must be paid off. The laws of the Universe demand this, so human beings 'choose' to undergo sufferings to repay this debt. There is no question of ever being forgiven this debt because 'God' is the sum total of us all, and 'It' is merely a Force. Therefore, we are responsible for our own illnesses and troubles, because we 'bring them on ourselves' in order to grow.[123] The NAM believes that since the human mind produces illness, it can also produce the cure![124] The doctrine of karma leads to fatalism, and sometimes to despair, for it may take several 'incarnations' to get free of one's problems, or one may be the eternal failure. People in the NAM refuse even to speak about death, as they fear it greatly.[125]

The NAM also teaches Pantheism, which states that not only can we say that we are part of God, but that individually and collectively we can claim to *be* God. Pantheism appears to be the result of submitting to ASC's, which was illustrated earlier. Nature and God are considered one. This view not only makes nature 'divine' but makes God 'natural'. Because of this, nature religions abound for those who are so inclined. This also rules out the supernatural and the miraculous for they are just the laws of nature that can be

44

explained scientifically, and when understood used to one's benefit.[126]

Variations on the theme are found in sun worship and nature worship, which are rampant. Ceremonies and rituals are performed for invoking the spirits of trees, animals, plants and mother earth, who is seen as a living being, worshipped as GAIA, a title taken from Greek mythology. This is done for purposes of healing, consciousness expansion and communion with the powers of the universe.[127]

The 'Earth Mother' deity is much more popular than the Heavenly Father, which smacks of male-dominated religions. The Heavenly Father requires sacrifice and a sacerdotal system to carry it out, but the Earth Mother allows one to celebrate life! As sociologist Robert Bellah sees it 'the sky religions emphasise the paternal, hierarchical, legalistic and ascetic, whereas the earth tradition emphasises the maternal, communal, expressive and joyful aspects of existence'.[128] One can see why Matthew Fox's *Creation Spirituality* is very important to them.[129]

This collective 'God' is spoken of as 'The Force' or 'Energy' or 'Consciousness', 'Infinite Intelligence', 'Principle' etc. It is not a moral Being to be worshipped as the Supreme One.[130] 'It' is impersonal and amoral, for one creates one's own morality. This force can be manipulated and used for one's own advantage, as we see in all the seminars where one is taught how to get wealth and material happiness from the 'universe' by the use of one's mental powers.[131]

Since the New Age teaches that we *are* God, there is therefore no sin, and no need for a Saviour. In consequence there is no forgiveness and no mercy. They deny that the seven sacraments have any value as means of grace, and they offer mind control techniques, psychology and other self-help answers to problems. Price puts this clearly: 'You are always expressing the idea of Who and What you are. If you think of yourself as a human being, you are going to experience that identity. But when you take the idea that you are a spiritual being, that you are God individualised, and begin to *live* that idea ... your whole world takes on a different tone and shape. Then he counsels his readers to assert: 'The Identity of God is individualised in me now. I am the Self-Expression of God. I am the Presence of God where I am. I am the Christ, Son of the Living God' (italics and capitals his).[132]

The repeated teaching of the NAM that we are perfect, autonomous, and self-sufficient gods, conditions its followers to specifically reject the teaching of Sacred Scripture that we are sinners, who are accountable to God for our behaviour, and that we are incapable of saving ourselves.[133] Referring to the Church's teaching, Price further states that 'there are some groups who continue to cling to the absurd idea that man is a miserable sinner and a worm of the dust', and he goes on to give his own interpretation of the Gospel that we were made sons of God, superior beings, and equal to Jesus.[134]

Counterfeit morality: the do-what-you-like system

'Create your own reality' is one of the catch phrases of the NAM. Morality is 'what you want', disregarding the needs of others or the justice of the situation. Adherents of the NAM use decrees, creative imagination, mantras, affirmations and occult invocations to create their own reality.[135] They do not accept that we are bound by God's moral law and they deny the reality of good and evil. Since we need to work out our karma, and we have many lives to lead, then objective evil can be seen in a different light.

Chandler quotes J. Z. Knight as saying that murder is not evil when one sees it in the light of reincarnation![136] He also quotes other examples to show how they justify abortion, while suicide is just a decision not to go on with this life but to choose another one to complete one's karma![137] The problem is that everything is relative because you create both your own reality and your own morality, so who is to say that your actions are evil? By what standard do you measure them? There is no authority to call upon that is recognised, or accepted by NAM. There are, therefore, no guidelines to one's behaviour, including one's sexual life, nor is any education accepted to inform the conscience.[138]

Another catch phrase is 'all is one'. Since there is no evil you can do as you like. Ramtha, J.Z. Knight's spirit guide, even tells his disciples that doing evil is good for them! After all, they can only

46

learn from experience! Since they believe that they are 'divine' anyway, no one can say that what they do is evil. This has produced the 'me generation' where there is no self-sacrifice, no giving, no generosity, but only hard, cruel self-indulgence.[139] Spangler complains of this, warning them that if they are always 'the consumer and never the consumed' that they 'end up with a bad case of spiritual anorexia'.[140]

The result of this type of teaching is breakdown in marriage and family.[141] The essential thing is that you care for yourself and your own growth. Other people, even family, are secondary.[142] Marilyn Ferguson admits that 'relationships are the crucible of the transformative process',[143] that one must go on with an appropriate partner, one that is synergistic, and holistic.[144] These 'soul partners' may be short lived.[145] Partners should not be possessive, as relationships should be open and 'free'.[146] She believes they are moving into a new family structure, namely the planetary family,[147] where children will not be 'owned' or even acknowledged by their biological parents. If people take these ideas seriously then social chaos follows. Baer claims that there is a high incidence of abortion in NAM circles. The ideal of unisex is widely aspired to, and generally there is free thinking on sexual ethics. Monumental self-centredness seems to be the trademark among so many who claim they are seeking 'higher things'![148]

Counterfeit prayer: communing with self or the unknown
The NAM offers a new spirituality. In fact, it is all about spiritual transformation.[149] Group meetings are often called 'prayer' meetings, which is confusing for the Christian. Each person must discover their 'Higher Self' or their own 'divinity'. They are encouraged to reach out for transcendental experiences in order to reach the new enlightenment – which is the discovery of their own divinity and their own unlimited potential. Any means that works to achieve this end is permitted. One of their catch-phrases is that if a thing works for you, it is for you!

Many of these groups abuse prayer techniques such as 'centreing'.They also use relaxation techniques, or mind control techniques in order to achieve 'peace' or quiet in mind and body. The centre is the self, not God, therefore there is no prayer. The purpose of achieving this relaxed mind and body is often for material gain in better work output in the market-place, or better health. Sometimes the pray-er wants 'spirituality' in out-of-the-body experiences which they call 'mysticism'. The means used to achieve altered states of consciousness are drugs, tarot cards, crystals, pendulums, yoga, TM, mantras, fasting, isolation, self-hypnosis, seances, and a form of mind control that is meditation on oneself and a programming of the mind.[150]

Counterfeit miracles

One of the very disturbing aspects of trance channelling is the phenomenon of psychic healing. In her book *The Beautiful Side of Evil* Johanna Michaelsen testifies to have been involved as an aide to a person involved in psychic healing. She claims to have witnessed astounding events, that could only be called 'miracles' to the onlooker. This raises the question of false miracles, or miracles coming from an evil source. Operations were carried out that amazed medical doctors, both as to the methods used, and the results achieved. The channelled spirit communicated with all those present and controlled the operations. Because this type of activity is not new or uncommon today, one must question the source. Do we accept healing at any price? Where is this power coming from? If it is not from God, do you want to allow some alien force to invade your personality?

Elliot Miller claims that 'Psychic healing has rapidly become accepted as a valid form of therapy in the medical world.' He says that a survey done in 1981 showed that fifty-eight per cent of medical school faculty members wanted psychic phenomena included in psychiatric training.[151] Pranic healing has also become very popular, even among Christians. This is based on the Hindu concept of 'prana' or 'universal life energy' which flows through the body. In a trance-like state the practitioner becomes a channel of universal life energy for the patient, who assimilates this energy (ibid.).

'Secular spirituality': It's all in the mind

For those who do not wish to enter into the new mysticism, there is another, more 'secular' type of New Age 'miracle' available. These people believe they can achieve anything through the controlled use of the energy of the mind and soul on the desired object. They teach that if you use a combination of positive thinking and creative imagination (or imaging) you can visualise and conceptualise the desired object with such intensity that you can objectify it in your life. For example, J. Randolph Price counsels his readers to contemplate 'Spirit appearing as lavish abundance' if you want money, or as 'restoring Power' if you desire healing. He also shows them how to get a life partner or a job. Whatever the need is 'the Power' out there will supply it.[152]

In other words, what you think in your mind you can create in the objective world around you![153] This is an insult to our Creator and a refusal of his divine providential care of our lives. When Job (42:2) received a new vision of God the Creator, he declared: 'I know that you are all-powerful, what you conceive, you can perform. I am the man who has obscured your designs with my empty-headed words'.

This claim to unlimited human potential is a claim to 'divinity'. New Age groups think that they can manipulate the forces in the Universe for their own ends, that through their own power they 'can make things happen'. Since they say that these forces are impersonal, one can use any technique that works to get the desired end. Thus the process is amoral. This is illustrated in the way one is told to use techniques to get a life partner, or to win millions in a lottery.[154] J.R. Price teaches us how to work with 'the Energy of the Absolute' and explains the lavish abundance that is there for you to tap when you get in touch with the Universal Energy.[155] Such an easy 'relationship' with God, where God's function is seen as supplying all our needs, shows the selfishness at the heart of this New Age.

All of this is a parody of Christian prayer and conversion to God, where we surrender our will to the holy will of God, and work with him to further his Kingdom on earth. It is also a denial of the place of suffering in the Christian life. Suffering and the Cross are seen to have no value, and so the one who is sick or suffering is condemned as having brought the condition upon themselves due

49

to their karmic state. These people want out-of-this-world experiences which have no reference to virtue, truth, morality, nor any commitment to God or one's neighbour.

One needs to realise that a concentration on the self is not prayer, even if some prayer techniques are used in the process. Christian prayer is reaching out to the true and only God in adoration, praise, repentance and petition for ourselves and for the rest of the world and its needs.

The New World Religion: NAM missionary policy

All the NAM authors teach that the Spirit Hierarchy have a master plan for planet Earth, which they operate in every age through their disciples, who influence the course of history. Creme calls these disciples today 'the new Group of World Servers'. They are working in every field, political, religious, social, scientific, educational and cultural, so their influence is felt everywhere. The Masters train them for their specific tasks, and 'their coming influence in world affairs will be great'.[156] What is afoot is the reconstruction of a new World Order, carried out by a group of high Initiates who are experts in every field.[157] The New Age social structures will come from these people.[158] This will lead inexorably towards a One World Government,[159] where high Initiates will be in charge.

Part of this plan is also a One World Church, which these writers refer to as the New World Religion. Alice Bailey speaks of this extensively.[160] The old forms of religion have to go in favour of the new form which will be one religion only,[161] as the new festivals 'will gradually supersede the festivals of the present world religions in the East and in the West.'[162] When the 'Christ' returns, he will assume spiritual rule in the hearts of everyone, everywhere. 'He has no place for the temples built in his name' as the simple Way to God that he taught has 'disappeared in the fogs of theology and the discussions of churchmen throughout the ages'. The great truths spoken by Christ on Earth have 'been lost in the labyrinths of the ecclesiastical minds which have sought to interpret them ... and have been superseded by the pomp and ceremony of elaborate rituals.[163] The New World Church will incorporate the teachings of ALL of the great world teachers and saviours.'[164]

50

What will happen to the religious organisations in the New World Order? Bailey says that 'the church movement, like all else, is but a temporary expedient and serves but a transient resting place for the evolving life. Eventually there will appear the Church Universal, and its definite outlines will appear towards the close of this century'.[165] Creme says that the 'purified churches' can be useful as places for teaching. He says that there will be a fusion of east and west, Christianity and Buddhism, plus the NAM teachings and the occult.[166]

'The Christian Churches can serve as a John the Baptist, as a voice crying in the wilderness, and as a nucleus through which world illumination may be accomplished.'[167] A warning note is then sounded: the Church is warned to 'show a wide tolerance, and teach no revolutionary doctrines nor cling to reactionary ideas.' Revolutionary doctrines are those which contradict the NAM *evolutionary doctrines*. Miller claims that Christian dogmatism is seen as definitely *anti-evolutionary*, and therefore a threat to global unity. Since they see this global unity as *survival* for humanity, it is not difficult to see that they would find justification for the elimination of this perceived threat.[168] Bailey reveals that the three main channels through which the New World Religion will accomplish its plans are the Church, The Masonic Fraternity, and the field of education.[169]

Why these three? The Church, because she has influence over the minds of millions of her adherents who accept all she says. The Masonic Fraternity, because it is occultic, and Bailey calls it 'the custodian of the law, the home of the Mysteries and the seat of initiation' (ibid.). The educational institutions because they are the means of teaching these new ideas to the public.[170] According to Bailey, the three paths leading to initiation are to be found among esotericists, the Church, and Masonry,[171] so they will be used as initiating centres for the New World Religion (ibid.).

She states further that all those 'souls on the Probationary Path or the Path of Discipleship today will be the nucleus of this new religion. They are to be 'gathered out of all the churches .. where they can consciously place their feet upon that Path which leads to the centre of peace' (ibid.). When this preparatory phase is over the great 'Mysteries will be restored to outward expression through the Church and the Masonic Fraternity.' Therefore she urges disciples today to teach the new ideas unceasingly.[172] This is being done through the multiplicity of seminars and courses that teach the NAM principles everywhere.

What would happen to the Church if she resisted this take-over? There are subtle hints in these NAM books that resistence will be crushed. Bailey says that the old forms will have to be destroyed to give way to the new.[173] The term 'old forms' means the Church as we know it today. She begins to describe new forms as the Ashrams.[174] The first point of the World Plan concerns the reorganisation of the World Religions in order to make of them one universal religion. It also includes a return of humanity to the simplicity of the Christ, and 'ridding the world of theology and ecclesiasticism'. The second stage is the destruction of orthodox Judaism, and the third lies in the reception of New Revelation.[175] The fourth and fifth stages seek to establish closer links with the Hierarchy, and then we move towards an era of peace.[176]

David Spangler, speaking through the entity 'Limitless Love and Truth', is quite open about the disasters that will accompany the death of the old and the birth of the New Age.[177] He says that 'this new humanity filled with my presence cannot be touched by whatever befalls the old. Should nuclear devices be used, the energies will be the revelation of me. All that will remain is what I am, and all that is not of me will disappear, to follow another law and another destiny.' This means that anyone remaining in the 'old order' will be sent off into death to continue their karmic journey to perfection! Of course we do not have to worry about this, as death has no meaning in this context.[178] Again he speaks of atomic power being released (ibid.), and tells his disciples not to worry, as war and destruction are all illusion anyway!

In chapter nine Spangler (through his entity) speaks of the relationship between the Old and the New Forms. The old must disintegrate, for it is already dead. 'It will move into greater states of confusion, of chaos, of destruction in the sense of disintegration.'[179] 'The presence of radioactivity upon the planet will render sterile all forms which cannot attune to new energies and will

52

make them incapable of reproducing themselves' (ibid.). 'The old will draw upon sources of energy which are intrinsically destructive and disintegrating'.[180] Of course 'it matters not what happens to the old...' (ibid.) as there 'is a sentence of absolute doom' upon the old forms (ibid.).

Why destroy the old? Well, 'the time for healing is past' and we must get on with building the New Forms.[181] Spangler says that 'if forms must be destroyed that this new presence be released then, so be it'.[182] The entity says that it is 'not ruthless' but wants to 'strike at the root cause' in order to change our thinking. There is no point 'in commiserating with the world's suffering' as you 'cannot heal a corpse' (ibid.). Finally, Spangler is told that these 'energies (of the Hierarchy) will in all ways seek to express through physical matter and ultimately will do so. If too great a stress of resistance to them is created, then the energies will work to shatter that resistance. If the resistance is in human consciousness, the new energies will remove that resistance within those human beings who have ceased to be nourished at the breast of the new heaven and the new earth.' Since this entity claims to be the source of the new heaven and new earth, it is speaking of those human beings who do not follow its guidance.[183]

One might conclude from this that the destruction 'of the old forms', namely the Church and Judaism, would come from 'on high' so to speak, but as we have already seen these entities work *through human beings.* Elliot Miller says that the Christian faith is incompatible with the global society that the NAM is working towards. 'There is no tolerable place for true Christianity' he claims. Because of the teachings on karma, death and evolution (to mention just a few) Miller says that the NAM which he calls 'The Aquarian Regime' would justify the persecution of Christians.[184]

Target areas for NAM evangelisation

The official language for this is 'planetisation' or 'globalism'. 'The Aquarian Conspiracy' is Marilyn Ferguson's term for the conscious effort by the NAM to 'win cultural dominance over secularism and traditional religion'.[185] Their target areas are health care, psychology, education, business and politics (ibid.). Miller reminds us that while there is no central organisation orchestrating the activities, it would 'be wrong to assume that there is no conscious collusion' between all the elaborate networks that feed into the same policies worldwide (ibid.).

Networking is essential to the NAM as its interests cover the whole of society. Since the 1970s networking has become *the way* that NAM mobilises its adherents with regard to numbers, but also to pool its resources. For example, those interested in politics work together; those interested in education collaborate, just as they do in health, social and religious matters. They contact each other through an international computer-based system called 'Peacenet' which acts as an information pool.[186]

NAM is targeting the schools: As Brooks Alexander has observed: 'In the ideological contest for cultural supremacy, public education is *the* prime target; it influences the most people in the most pervasive way at the most impressionable age. No other social institution has anything close to the same potential for mass indoctrination'.[187] The infiltration of education began in the 1960s with the introduction of 'humanistic' elements. This was followed in the 1970s with 'transpersonal' or 'holistic' education. By 1980 Marilyn Ferguson could write that 'the deliberate use of consciousness-expanding techniques in education, only recently well under way, is now in mass schooling'.[188] Children are taught 'right brain' activities such as meditation, Yoga, guided imagery, chanting, and fantasy role-playing games. Children are, therefore being led into psychic experiences on the premise that this will improve their performance in learning, and help them to gain control and remain calm (ibid.). Of course there is nothing wrong with meditation, guided imagery and role-playing if the teaching is Christian both in content and in direction.[189]

The need for discernment
Christians have had to discern false prophets and teachers from the beginning of the Church. False doctrine is nothing new. Both Jesus himself, and the early Church teachers warned us of this. The Apostle John warns us: 'It is not every spirit, my dear people, that you

can trust; test them, to see if they come from God, there are many false prophets, now, in the world.

'You can tell the spirits that come from God by this: every spirit which acknowledges that Jesus, the Christ has come in the flesh is from God; but any spirit which will not say this of Jesus is not from God, but is the spirit of Antichrist, whose coming you were warned about' (I Jn 4:1-3).

Paul also warned the Thessalonians to 'test everything and hold on to what is good and shun every form of evil' (I Th 5:21). Jesus warned us about counterfeit Christs in Matthew 24:5 and counterfeit prophets in Matthew 7:1-20. We read in Mark 13:21-23: 'If anyone says to you then, "Look, here is the Christ" or, "Look, he is there", do not believe it; for false christs and false prophets will arise and produce signs and portents to deceive the elect, if that were possible. You must therefore be on your guard. I have forewarned you of everything'.

Jesus laid down the principle that we would recognise them by their fruits. If they remove themselves from revealed truth, holiness, and obedience to God's will and word then do not follow them. If they remove themselves from the Church founded by Christ, then they are false prophets. We must continuously question what is *the source* of this new teaching, or these so-called miracles or signs. If the source is not God, as he has revealed himself in the Holy Scriptures, then it is counterfeit, even if it appears to be good.

The doctrine of reincarnation has become very popular, with people testifying to 'other lives' when they regress under hypnosis. Some people even offer detailed information about their 'past lives'. One must ask how this happens, and what is going on. Are our minds being manipulated to produce 'evidence', or is reincarnation *fact?* The Scriptures are quite clear that reincarnation does not occur, no matter what these people claim. Hebrews 9:27 states that 'human beings die only once, after which comes judgment'. I Thessalonians 4:13-14 states that we can 'be *quite certain* about those who have died, to make sure that you do not grieve about them, like the other people who have no hope. We believe that Jesus died and rose again, and that it will be *the same* for those who have died in Jesus: God will bring them *with him.*' Paul's glorious passage in I Corinthians 15:35-58 explains the manner of our resurrection. He concludes the passage with this triumphant burst of praise: 'When this perishable nature of ours puts on imperishability, and when this mortal nature has put on immortality, then the words of scripture will come true: Death is swallowed up in victory ... let us thank God for giving us the victory through our Lord, Jesus Christ.'

Jesus, gave us the truth about death, forgiveness and mercy. In II Corinthians 5:17 Paul tells us that Jesus makes 'a new creation' even in this life, and eternal joy in Heaven follows it. This is the Good News of Christianity. The doctrine of the Resurrection is in complete contradiction to that of reincarnation. Reincarnation says that the body is not important. It is just the vehicle you have chosen in which you want to learn some lessons. Romans 8:11 and 8:18-22 tells us that our body, and eventually all creation, participates in Redemption. Our bodies will be raised up on the Last Day to join us for ever in glory.

When groups claim that they can heal at a distance, or by clairvoyance, we must ask 'By what power is this done?' (see Ac 4:7). Is that power human and natural or is it from the occult (even if veiled by modern terminology or techniques), or is it from God? If the source is God, then the healing will further the eternal salvation of that individual who received the gift. It will being peace of soul, grace and a desire to serve God. If it is from an evil source it brings disquiet, unease, and pushes the person away from God and his Church towards self-deception, or sometimes attracts the person to the occult.

When we are invited to a 'prayer meeting' it is now necessary, unfortunately, to ask if it is a Christian group, as many NAM groups call their weekly get-togethers 'prayer' meetings, even though their activities concentrate on the self. So one must question what is going on at the meeting. Find out who or what is the 'god' or 'source' being contacted. Ask to know the theology and doctrines of the teachers. Enquire about their holy books, and then seek advice from competent persons, for these groups sometimes go under the heading of meditation groups, but the meditation is not on God. Christian meditation concentrates on the Life, Passion,

Death and Resurrection of Jesus so that we can grow in his likeness. It requires no initiation ceremony, as does TM, but it is good to receive spiritual direction from a competent person.

One must question also why the NAM is so hostile to revealed truth. NAM leaders say that it accepts the Bible, but only conditionally, as one holy book among others. It is not absolute truth, nor do they accept that it has any more authority than other ancient books, whether accepted as inspired by other religions or not. NAM not only picks and chooses what it likes from the Bible, but also reinterprets the passages it selects and gives them the NAM metaphysical slant.[190] Texe Marrs in *Dark Secrets of the New Age* agrees that the NAM rejects Christian doctrine as intolerant, because it claims to be *the* truth.[191]

NAM rejects Christian Revelation, and at the same time teaches the doctrines of the occult mysteries as if they were truth. Their teaching on Lucifer as 'The Light' applies the attributes of God to Satan, who is worshipped as God. Jesus referred to Satan as 'the prince of this world' in John 12:31; 14:30. He called the reign of this prince 'the reign of darkness' in Luke 22:53. Hence we can see the spiritual darkness of the best-known teachers of the NAM, who are convincing others that this rejection of the truth of Revelation is somehow 'enlightenment'! Let us remember the warning of Scripture in Isaiah 5:20: 'Woe to those who call evil good, and good evil, who substitute darkness for light, and light for darkness....'

Worship of self: the new idolatry

Every age has had its idols. The Scriptures bear abundant testimony to the fact that people have a tendency to deviate in matters of worship. In the Old Testament whenever the Lord seemed to be very quiet, or the people lost faith in their religious leaders, they turned to pagan practices and idol worship. Sometimes they even mixed the worship of God with pagan rites when they were very confused. And these rites usually involved some form of the occult. The prophets spoke out boldly against these deviations in order to help the people to remain in a true relationship with God.

Today the same phenomenon is occurring, and we need to be alert to it, for fear we get sucked into something that cuts us off from our saving relationship to Jesus Christ our *only* Saviour. The temptation today is the worship of self. J.R. Pice has a chapter headed: 'The All-in-All of Self' which says it all.[192] We have become so impressed by our own progress that we feel that we can save ourselves also! Society is so absorbed with health, fitness, food, recreation, holidays abroad and fashion, often to the detriment of the spiritual life. When we do become aware of the void this creates, we turn to material things and dangerous techniques in order to have 'peace of mind'. This shows that we have set our hearts on the world, and not on God's Kingdom. We have forgotten that 'we do not have here a lasting city' (Hb 13:14).

Jesus teaches us in Luke 12:22-31 that life is more important than food, and the body is more important than clothes. He says that if we set our hearts on his Kingdom that God will see to our needs according to his Divine Providence. Our tendency today to live life in independence of God could have eternal consequences for us. God wants to be Father, Redeemer, Saviour, Healer, and Sanctifier to his children who are in dire need of these gifts from him. If we refuse this saving relationship with God then we frustrate his loving designs for us as individuals, but also for the furthering of his Kingdom on earth.

NOTES

(Full details of the publications referred to in these notes can be found in the Select Bibliography, pp. 79-80).

1.   *Psychology as Religion: The Cult of Self-Worship*, by Paul Vitz.
2.   *The Aquarian Conspiracy*, Marilyn Ferguson, chapters 1,3, 7, 10, 11. This book is a compendium of the New Age agenda & philosophical vision, and is considered the unofficial 'scripture' of NAM.
3.   *The Aquarian Conspiracy*, Marilyn Ferguson, p. 19.
4.   'New Age Science and the Challenge of Discernment', William Thompson, pp. 82-88 in *Reimagination of the World*, David Spangler & William Thompson. Science is spiritualised & glorified on p. 23.

5. *Understanding the New Age*, Russell Chandler, p. 43.
6. Ibid., pp. 44-45.
7. *Understanding the New Age*, Russell Chandler, ch.5.
8. *Understanding the New Age*, Russell Chandler, p. 44.
9. Even William Thompson speaks about the 'sloppy syncretism of the NAM in the 70s'; p. 13 of *Reimagination of the World*. This book is a critique of the NAM by two prominent NAM leaders. It covers the papers given at two seminars on various topics.
10. Quote from Carl A. Raschke in 'Interruption of Eternity; modern Gnosticism in the origins of the new religious Consciousness' in *Understanding the New Age*, Russell Chandler, p. 45.
11. *The Aquarian Conspiracy: Personal & Social Transformation in the 1980s*, Marilyn Ferguson, pp. 128-134.
12. *Reimagination of the World*, David Spangler/William Thompson, p. 19.
13. *The Reappearance of the Christ and the Masters of Wisdom*, B. Creme, p. 86-87.
14. *Understanding the New Age*, Russell Chandler, p. 47. Helena Blavatsky's major work is called *The Secret Doctrine*. It has two volumes: 1. *Cosmogenesis*, and 2. *Anthropogenesis*. They were published in 1888. The teachings of the major NAM writers are found in these books. B. Creme says on p. 107 of *The Reappearance of Christ and The Masters of Wisdom* that the material was dictated to Blavatsky by the entity known as the Master D.K., the same one responsible for the works of Alice Bailey later. He also says that the Agni Yoga Teachings were given to Helena Roerich by the same spirit entity. Therefore *the source* of all this material is from the spirit world!
15. For a 'Who's Who' of writers and thinkers of the NAM see *Straight Answers on the New Age*, Bob Larson, ch. 12. It also lists some of the most important NAM Foundations.
16. *Reimagination of the World*, David Spangler/William Thompson, p.10.
17. *A Crash Course in the New Age Movement*, Elliot Miller, p. 89.

18. Ibid., pp. 89-127. He was formerly involved in the NAM, and gives a balanced clear exposition of it and its effects on the political, social and religious scene in America. He is very clear on NAM politics.

19. 'The Bringing Forth of Worlds', p. 175, an article in *Reimagination of the World*, David Spangler / William Thompson.

20. 'Sixteen Years into New Age', p. 15, an article in *Reimagination of the World*, David Spangler / William Thompson.

21. *Reappearance of Christ & the Masters of Wisdom*, Benjamin Creme, p. 46.

22. 'The Self and the Other', an article by William Thompson in *Reimagination of the World*, David Spangler/ William Thompson.

23. *Reimagination of the World*, David Spangler/ William Thompson, p.112.

24. Ibid., p. 113.

25. *New Age From a Biblical Viewpoint*, M. Basilea Schlink.

26. *Externalisation of the Hierarchy*, Alice A. Bailey, p. 33.

27. Ibid., p. 355.

28. Ibid., p. 542.

29. Ibid., p. 543.

30. Ibid., p. 545.

31. Ibid., p. 544.

32. *Reimagination of the World*, David Spangler/ William Thompson.

33. Ibid., p. 175.

34. Ibid., p. 176.

35. *Reappearance of Christ and the Masters of Wisdom*, B. Creme, p. 67.

36. *Confronting The New Age*, Douglas Groothuis, p. 107.

37. *Reappearance of Christ and The Masters of Wisdom*, Benjamin Creme, p. 116.

38. *Inside the New Age Nightmare*, Randall N. Baer, a former top NAM leader in the USA: *Reimagination of the World*, David Spangler/William Thompson, p. 29.

39. *Externalisation of the Hierarchy*, Alice Bailey, pp. 472-576.

40. *Reimagination of the World*, David Spangler/William

Thompson, p. 206, where Spangler speaks about this 'John'. See also: *Understanding the New Age*, Russell Chandler, p. 54-55. *A Crash Course in the New Age*, Elliot Miller, p. 141-182. In this book Miller gives both the background and an analysis of this phenomenon. Like Chandler, he is inclined to give more psychological weight to the activity of channelling, than to accept that it is purely demonic activity.

41. *Inside the New Age Nightmare*, Randall N. Baer, p. 103.
42. Ibid., and p. 175 of *Reimagination of the World*, David Spangler/ William Thompson.
43. *Understanding the New Age*, Russell Chandler, p. 254.
44. *Revelation: The Birth of a New Age*, David Spangler. The theme of the whole book is enlightenment from these Masters.
45. *A Crash Course in the NAM*, Elliot Miller, pp. 217-223. *Inside the New Age Nightmare*, Randall N. Baer, pp. 1-22. Both of them used drugs to achieve altered states of consciousness.
46. *Inside the New Age Nightmare*, Randall N. Baer, pp. 103-4. See also *The Beautiful Side of Evil* by Johanna Michaelson, who was personal assistant to a psychic surgeon in Mexico for fourteen months, witnessed astounding feats which were acclaimed as miracles, and then went on to discern their source.
47. *Inside the New Age Nightmare*, Randall N. Baer, p. 99.
48. *A Crash Course in the NAM*, Elliot Miller, p.169.
49. Ibid., p. 155.
50. *Straight Answers On The New Age*, Bob Larson, ch. 5.
51. *Inside the New Age Nightmare,* Randall N. Baer, p. 20. See also *Understanding the New Age*, Russell Chandler, ch. 9.
52. *Anthropogenesis*: volume two of *The Secret Doctrine*, Helena Blavatsky, p. 641.
53. *Inside the New Age Nightmare*, Randall N. Baer, p. 105. Elliot Miller, in *A Crash Course in the New Age Movement*, says that the NAM has an occult spirituality that is repugnant to, and incompatible with the Christian faith. See pp. 122, 173. See also *Unicorn in the Sanctuary*, Randy England. His book shows the impact of the NAM on the Catholic Church, p. 117.

54. *Dark Secrets of the New Age*, Texe Marrs, p. 11. See also Randall N. Baer, p. 9.
55. *Beyond The Love Game*, Robert Scheid, 1980, where these principles are applied to getting a life partner.
See also *The Secret Place*, Richard E. McKenzie, 1984, which explains the gateways to the subconscious used by the Silva Mind Control. They teach that the mind can be programmed to achieve any goal.
56. *Revelation: The Birth of a New Age*, David Spangler, p. 14.
57. Ibid., p. 49.
58. Ibid., pp. 40-43.
59. Ibid., pp. 33-38.
60. Ibid., p. 50.
61. Ibid., p. 37.
62. Ibid., p. 48.
63. Ibid., p. 50.
64. *Reappearance of Christ and the Masters of Wisdom*, B. Creme pp. 227-248.
65. *Dark Secrets of the New Age*, Texe Marrs, p. 28.
66. *Reflections of the Christ*, David Spangler, pp. 40-44. Spangler claims that this book was dictated to him by spirit entities.
67. Ibid., pp. 36-39.
68. *Dark Secrets of the New Age*, Texe Marrs, p. 75. See also *Reimagination of the World*, Spangler/Thompson, pp.148-155.
69. *Dark Secrets of the New Age*, Texe Marrs pp. 79-83.
70. Ibid., pp. 75,76.
71. *Reimagination of the World*, David Spangler/William Thompson, p. 133.
72. Ibid., p. 175.
73. *Reappearance of Christ and The Masters of Wisdom*, Benjamin Creme, p. 135.
74. Ibid., p. 75.
75. *Externalisation of the Hierarchy*, Alice Bailey, p. 107.
76. *Anthropogenesis*, Helena Blavatsky, p. 107.
77. Ibid., p. 508.

78. Ibid., further quotation from Eliphas Levi, p. 510.
79. Ibid., p. 511.
80. *Anthropogenesis*, Helena Blavatsky p. 512.
81. Ibid., p. 513.
82. *The Planetary Commission*, John R. Price, pp. 32-46.
83. Ibid., pp. 25-26.
84. *Rays and Initiations*, Alice Bailey.
85. *Inside the New Age Nightmare*, Randall N. Baer, p. 107.
86. *Reappearance of the Christ and the Masters of Wisdom*, B. Creme, p. 29.
87. *Rays and Initiations*, Alice Bailey, p. 26.
88. See *The Externalisation of the Hierarchy*, Alice Bailey, p. 86 for material on Lord Maitreya.
    See also *Straight Answers on the New Age*, Bob Larson, pp. 198-200; *Inside the New Age Nightmare*, Randall N. Baer p. 43.
89. *Reappearance of Christ and the Masters of Wisdom*, B. Creme, pp. 227-248.
90. Ibid., p. 28.
91. Ibid., p. 115.
92. *Externalisation of the Hierarchy*, Alice Bailey, pp. 591-612.
93. Ibid., p. 597.
94. *Reimagination of the World*, David Spangler, p. 137.
95. Ibid., p. 141.
96. Ibid., p. 148.
97. *Revelation: The Birth of a New Age*, David Spangler, pp. 102-109.
98. *Reappearance of Christ and the Masters of Wisdom*, Benjamin Creme, p. 30.
99. Ibid., p. 31.
100. Ibid., p. 47.
101. Ibid., pp. 137-139.
102. Ibid., p. 46.
103. Ibid., p. 64.
104. Ibid., p. 54.
105. Ibid., p. 108.
106. *Dark Secrets of the New Age*, Texe Marrs, p. 89

See also *The Planetary Commission*, John Randolph Price pp. 24-27. He is a co-founder with his wife of the Quartus Foundation, a major NAM enterprise. He uses Christian language throughout the book to put across unChristian principles of living.

107. *Reappearance of Christ and the Masters of Wisdom*, Benjamin Creme, pp. 39-41.
108. 1. The Light: See pages 33-36 of chapter 3.
    2. The Christ: See pages 37-40 of chapter 3.
    3. The Masters: See pages 29-31 of chaper 3.
    4. God: See pages 29, 33, 44, 45, 46 of chapter 3.
    5. 'The centre where the Will of God is known' is called Shamballa: See pages 34-35 of chapter 3.
109. *Inside the New Age Nightmare*, Randall N. Baer, p. 84.
110. Ibid., p. 86.
111. *The Aquarian Conspiracy*, Marilyn Ferguson pp. 241, 414.
112. Ibid., p. 414.
113. Ibid., pp. 415, 423.
114. *A Crash Course in NAM*, Elliot Miller, p. 36.
115. Ibid., p. 37.
116. *Confronting the New Age*, Douglas Groothuis, p. 31.
117. See *Revelation: The Birth of a New Age*, David Spangler. See also *The Rays and Initiations* and *The Externalisation of the Hierarchy*, both by Alice A. Bailey. These are just some of the works containing the 'new revelation'.
118. *The Aquarian Conspiracy*, Marilyn Ferguson, p. 403.
119. Ibid., pp. 402, 404, 406, 407.
120. *Inside the New Age Nightmare*, Randall N. Baer, pp. 65, 69.
121. *Dark Secrets of the New Age*,Texe Marrs, p. 146.
122. *Anthropogenesis*, Helena Blavatsky, p. 484.
123. *Understanding the New Age*, Russell Chandler, p. 168.
124. *The Aquarian Conspiracy*, Marilyn Ferguson, pp. 264-305.
125. Ibid., p. 442-443.
126. *A Crash Course in New Age*, Elliot Miller pp. 37-51. In this section he shows how the NAM is trying to be scientific about its activities. It desperately wants a marriage with science, for this would 'prove' its theories, and prove the Church wrong.

127. *Inside the New Age Nightmare*, Randall N. Baer, pp. 115,116.
128. *A Crash Course in the New Age*, Elliot Miller, p. 30.
129. *Understanding the New Age*, Russell Chandler, p. 209; *Dark Secrets of the New Age*, Texe Marrs, p. 79.
130. *Confronting the New Age*, Douglas Groothuis, p. 22.
131. *Inside the New Age Nightmare*, Randall N. Baer, pp. 128-132.
132. *The Planetary Commission*, John Randolph Price, p. 81.
133. *Inside the New Age Nightmare*, Randall N. Baer, p. 115.
134. *The Planetary Commission*, John Randolph Price, p. 162.
135. *Confronting the New Age*, Douglas Groothuis, p 24 ; Randall N. Baer, p. 115.
136. *Understanding the New Age*, Russell Chandler, p. 287.
137. *Inside the New Age Nightmare*, Randall N. Baer, p. 116.
138. Ibid., p. 288-291. See also p. 126.
139. *Inside the New Age Nightmare*, Randall N. Baer, pp. 128-132.
140. *Reimagination of the World*, David Spangler/William Thompson, p. 53.
141. Ibid., p.124.
142. Ibid., See also *The Aquarian Conspiracy*, Marilyn Ferguson chapter 12, where she acknowledges that the NAM causes marital breakdown as people need to go on with 'suitable' partners, even if temporary. The partners must have 'synergy' for that period: pp. 206, 431-432.
143. Ferguson p. 427; for marriage breakdown, pp. 429-430.
144. Ibid., p. 431-2.
145. Ibid., p. 437; See Randall N. Baer pp. 24-25. He had a 'soul mate' for some years.
146. *The Aquarian Conspiracy*, M. Ferguson, p. 433.
147. Ibid., pp. 442-3.
148. *Inside the New Age Nightmare*, Randall N. Baer, pp.125-127
149. 'Images of New Age' in *Reimagination of the World*, pp. 29-33. Spangler admits that spirituality & transformation are the goals of NAM.
150. *Inside the New Age Nightmare*, Randall N. Baer, p. 102.
151. *A Crash Course in The New Age*, Elliot Miller, p. 93.
152. *The Planetary Commission*, John Randolph Price, p. 96.

153. *The Secret Place*, Richard E. McKenzie, and *Beyond the Love Game*, Robert Scheid.
154. *Inside the New Age Nightmare*, Randall N. Baer, pp. 115, 135.
155. *The Planetary Commission*, John Randolph Price, pp. 100-103 and p. 117-124.
156. *Reappearance of Christ and the Masters of Wisdom*, Benjamin Creme.
157. Ibid., p. 34.
158. Ibid., p. 35.
159. Ibid., pp. 167-169.
160. *Externalisation of the Hierarchy*, Alice Bailey, from p. 400.
161. Ibid., p. 401.
162. Ibid., p. 402.
163. Ibid., p. 403.
164. Ibid., pp. 406-422.
165. Ibid., p. 510.
166. *Reappearance of Christ and the Masters of Wisdom*, Benjamin Creme, pp. 84-89.
167. *Externalisation of the Hierarchy*, Alice Bailey, p. 510.
168. *A Crash Course in the New Age*, Elliot Miller, p. 122.
169. *Externalisation of the Hierarchy*, Alice Bailey, p. 511.
170. Ibid., p. 512.
171. Ibid., p. 513.
172. Ibid., pp. 514-517.
173. Ibid., p. 518.
174. Ibid., p. 519.
175. Ibid., p. 551.
176. Ibid., p. 552.
177. *Revelation: Birth of a New Age*, David Spangler, p. 64.
178. Ibid., p. 65.
179. Ibid., p. 74.
180. Ibid., p. 75.
181. Ibid., p. 76.
182. Ibid., p. 77.
183. Ibid., p. 79.
184. *A Crash Course in the New Age*, Elliot Miller, p. 122.

185. Ibid., p. 90.
186. One computerised network which furnishes access to people, research and places is Box 18666, Denver, Colorado 80218. Tel: (303) 832-9264; also Nucleus, 188 Old Street, London EC1. Tel: 01-250-1219. This is a data bank on more than 6,000 NAM groups in the UK. An extensive list of addresses for NAM Foundations and networks is found in *The Aquarian Conspiracy*, Marilyn Ferguson pp. 465-471.
187. Ibid., p. 95.
188. Ibid., pp. 95-98.
189. Ibid.,
190. See *Inside the New Age Nightmare*, Randall N. Baer, p. 61.
See also a reinterpretation of Christ by David Spangler in *Reimagination of the World* pp. 136-147. It is a discussion paper on the Cosmic Christ, and he makes it clear that he is not referring to the historical Jesus of Nazareth in any way. He is speaking about our own evolution to the 'Christ' status. It is definitely a 'new gospel and a new Christ' as St Paul condemned in Galatians 1.
191. *Dark Secrets of the New Age*, Texe Marrs, p. 45.
192. *The Planetary Commission*, John Randolph Price, pp. 92-96.

4

QUESTIONS PEOPLE ASK REGARDING
NEW AGE ACTIVITIES

There are many questions asked today by concerned Christians, confronted with aspects of the NAM in everyday life. Some of these questions will be touched upon here, and treated in a simple way.

Reflexology

This is press point therapy applied to the feet in a type of foot massage. Many Christians are using it with good effect to help reduce tension and stimulate healing. When carried out by a competent person who is properly trained, such as a nurse, it can be quite beneficial. But when it is done in seminars given by NAM people, you will be also offered the philosophy of the NAM. You will be told that the relaxation achieved does not last unless you are handling your other life problems, which is true. Then you are invited to join in other NAM exercises and the reflexology becomes an entrance into the NAM for you.

Samuel Pfeifer MD has written a book called *Healing at any Price?* (1988). It deals with the hidden dangers of alternative medicine. In chapter 5 he deals with reflexology, calling it 'laying hands on the feet'! He points out that the origins of reflexology go back to Chinese and Indian traditional medicine. Therefore it was developed out of the philosophy that is the source of acupuncture. As a medical doctor he challenges the theory of the energy zones in the feet, but believes that there are psychological reasons why the therapy has a good effect on the patient. After all, they are cared for delicately and personally by a compassionate person for an hour, and many people would lack, and feel the need for this kind of personal attention. Besides, the action in itself is soothing, and therefore helpful to the stressed person.

Acupuncture

This comes from ancient Chinese medicine. It is discussed by Samuel Pfeifer in chapter 4 of his book. This is the use of needles to stimulate healing in a wide range of illnesses, and also to enable people to have an operation without an anaesthetic. It operates on the Chinese concept of the life energy or Chi (often referred to in Yoga circles here in Ireland as Ki). The philosophical thinking behind acupuncture comes from Taoism and the concept of Yin and Yang, and of being at one with the forces in the universe through meditation.

Pfeifer quotes the Taoist philosopher George Ohsawa, the father of macrobiotics, as saying that 'oriental medicine cannot be separated from its philosophical underpinnings' (p. 32). Yet he shows that western therapists think that they can turn acupuncture into a purely 'pins and needles' affair. The NAM has no difficulty with acupuncture because it accepts the eastern philosophy behind it. But what about Christians? Can they accept the help and not be affected by its religious content? Many believe they can. The general principle in this matter is that these practices are not bad in themselves, and dissociated from their original context can be practiced by Catholics with due discretion.

Pfeifer also challenges the results of acupuncture. He says that the results of scientific tests are confusing, indicating that the results are coming from a variety of factors, including a patient's belief in the therapist. If you are interested in acupuncture then read up on the subject and have an informed opinion on it. Do not allow NAM groups to use it to 'rope you in' to their way of life.

Transcendental Meditation

This has been popular in various forms for a long time. What are we to make of it? In his book *TM: A Cosmic Confidence Trick*, by John Allan, we find the practice analysed and its dangers pointed out. TM has come to us from India. It was passed on from Guru Dev to his devoted follower Maharishi. When Guru Dev died in 1953, Maharishi went into seclusion for two years. He then emerged to found an International Academy of Meditation near the Himalayas. There he developed a worldwide strategy to spread

TM around the globe. From then on he was called Maharishi (meaning 'great sage') Mahesh (his family name) Yogi (meaning: 'united with God'). He travelled to America and began, after some initial difficulties, the fastest-growing cult in the west. By 1972 it had 500 conversions per month in Britain alone. John Allan claims that by 1980 75,000 Britons had been *initiated* into TM, which was, by then, a movement in its own right.

TM is ancient Brahmanism and Hinduism. God is seen as the impersonal Brahman, and it is very important to open up to this Being. It teaches that the world is just *maya* or illusion, and so it is harmful to get too deeply involved in the affairs of the world. There are many ways to open up to this being, through many forms of *yoga*. The Maharishi advocates *bhakti yoga* as the discipline of devotion. The technique for showing devotion is meditation, a type of meditation that transcends ordinary consciousness, and lifts our awareness to a higher level. One must work to achieve 'cosmic consciousness' whereby one can be completely at rest in the midst of a hectic life. No wonder so many want to try it out! The danger that is not pointed out is that *in this state* of so-called cosmic consciousness people are open to spirit influences without being in control, for they have surrendered to this 'consciousness'.

Initiation into TM involves the *puja* ceremony, which the TM teacher carries out on behalf of the pupil. The pupil is assured that this is *not* a religious ceremony, even though they must bring the traditional gifts, namely, fruit, flowers, a fee, and a white handkerchief. These gifts are then dedicated by the teacher in a simple Sanskrit ceremony before the teaching begins. During this ceremony the teacher and pupil sit before an altar covered with the white cloth on which there is a picture of Guru Dev, a candle, incense, as well as other objects.

The pupil is warned not to speak about the ceremony to anyone. The gifts are laid on the altar and dedicated. Incense is offered to the picture of the Guru. A long litany in Sanskrit is then chanted, calling on the Hindu Pantheon and Guru Dev. The pupil is invited to join in the chant with the new mantra, which is given during the ceremony. The mantra is used to bring people down into the emptiness of their being. The silent repetition of this sound causes psychic vibrations which affect the meditator's mental and physiological functioning.[1]

TM specialists insist that the Puja ceremony is *the power* behind TM! In her major work *The Externalisation of the Hierarchy* (eighth printing 1989; pp. 144-145), Alice Bailey says that the true mantra is OM. This is the 'Sacred Word' even though 'there are several such mantric formulas and Words of Power'. When used correctly they 'automatically become dynamically effective' she says, and 'they will produce changes in the person and their circumstances in life.' Alice Bailey is speaking out of an occult background where the mantra is known and used properly.

The puja ceremony involves breaking the First Commandment which forbids us to call upon strange or false gods. It is also an initiation into Hinduism, which the unsuspecting Christian may not realise. Nevertheless Maharishi denies that TM has anything to do with religion! He has tried to present it to the western mind as a purely scientific technique, but the scientific claims are hard to prove.

TM is, therefore, not something that a Catholic can be involved in. We have a long tradition of Christian meditation, which brings us into union with God. Remain with Jesus, the *only* Saviour. Guru Dev is nobody's saviour, not even his own![2]

Yoga

Yoga classes are presented all over Ireland and have an immense popularity. They are presented as physical exercises for the sake of health, wholeness, slimming, or a variety of other reasons. Many Christians refuse to see anything in Yoga apart from the physical aspects of it. But let us look closer.

The eastern religions can be called the Yogic Tradition, and it originated in India, the home of the gurus. The main themes of this tradition are transcendentalism and the spiritual journey. The Yogic world view is tied up with their belief in the law of karma which traps people into the cycle of suffering and evil. One needs to seek liberation from karma through the disciplines of Yoga, which involve the discipline of the body in exercises and

71

diet to liberate the true 'life force' and set one on this road to enlightenment. Reincarnation and karma are basic beliefs in the yogic tradition. The idea of reincarnation is expressed by westerners as remembering so-called 'past lives' , and the need to find the 'soul mate' who helps one on the freedom trail.[3]

'Yoga' literally means 'to bind together', to 'hold fast' or 'to yoke'. The word is used to describe any ascetic technique involving the type of meditation which is TM. The idea that Yoga was good for your health was developed in the 1960s in order to get the materialistic west interested and involved in Hinduism. In fact, it was the way the gurus set out 'to evangelise' the west.[4]

Yoga and TM go hand-in-hand as one system. Any serious Yogi will admit this. The physical exercises by themselves have only limited value, but when combined to TM they initiate one into full-blown Hinduism. The full package is Yoga, TM and holistic living. An essential ingredient is a guru, as one cannot embark on this journey into the unknown alone. One must be guided by a more experienced person in order to deal with the pitfalls. One must be 'converted' to this way of life, as many Irish people have in the past ten years, due to groups like the Tony Quinn Yoga groups.

Astrology

Astrology has found a new popularity with the arrival of Hinduism into the west. A newspaper without one's 'stars' is unusual nowadays. One even finds astrologers being consulted regarding political events as we saw on Sky News during the 1992 British elections, and the astrologers got it right where the opinion polls got it wrong! They said that John Major's chart showed good signs for him, but not for the opposition. Consulting one's stars is part of the Yogic system of belief. There are essentially two forms of it. Natal astrology deals with individuals. Mundane astrology deals with world events and history. Accepting astrology reinforces the belief in the law of karma, as your chart may have 'good' or 'bad' signs for you right now, and this may apply to a country also.

Astrology was important in the ancient world, but Christianity dealt strongly with it, and for centuries it died down. It revived in Europe in the latter half of the nineteenth century with the rise of Theosophy, but it had remained popular in China, India and the Islamic world. It did not revive in the west until the twentieth century, but it has gained steadily in popularity ever since, with polls claiming that forty per cent of Americans now believe in it.

The claims of astrology have been thoroughly discredited by scientific research. The physical planets in the Universe do not direct and guide the lives of living beings, for they are non-living objects. Astrology belongs to the occult and the magic arts.[5]

Many Christians seems to think that it is harmless to consult an astrologer, and to follow the 'stars' in one's everyday life. This is not so, for one is being guided by a false system of mythology and ancient so-called 'gods'. For many it is the beginning of a journey that leads into the occult proper, and into other NAM activities that are dangerous to one's spiritual life. It also rejects the teaching of Jesus and the Church that we should trust Divine Providence in our daily lives. The need to know one's stars seems to stem from a need to have something in our lives under control when there is so much happening all around us that is not in our control.

New Age music

There are hundreds of tapes of NAM music available, which many people enjoy without realising that it *is* NAM music. They just enjoy the sound. However, this is not why many of these tapes are made! They are made to help one in the meditative process, and there are sounds that are meant to affect the mind. It is debatable whether they are harmful in themselves, however. New Age music tapes can be recognised by their covers, very often, for they illustrate mythological and druidic themes. They also deal with themes of relaxation of mind and body.

Elliot Miller has a balanced discussion of NAM music in his book *A Crash Course in the New Age* (pp. 190-192). He says that there are different types of NAM music available. One type consists of music deliberately constructed to help 'build a bridge between the conscious and the subconscious' such as that of

Swiss harpist Andreas Vollenweider, just to give one example. There is also the type that 'gets on the bandwagon' for the sake of financial gain or even artistic expression, but may not have any commitment to the NAM, or to persuading people to join it. Then there are the 'evangelistic types' who want to convert people through the medium of music, and they usually run seminars helping people to enter into ASCs (altered states of consciousness) through the help of the music.

If the NAM music is without words it is debatable whether the authors can affect the consciousness of the listener, as the listener may just enjoy the sound without going any further. But if the music has the mantra OM in it, and, the mantra is chanted or given in a meditative, rhythmic way, then one realises that one is being led into NAM ASCs. Every listener must make up their own mind on the subject, and not allow an invasion of their privacy. We must be wary, and discern.

There are also video cassettes available called 'Video Hypnosis'. They are meant to be used for self-hypnosis for gaining self-confidence, losing weight, relaxation, accelerated learning etc. It should be superfluous to point out the dangers of self-hypnosis, for whatever reason, for how can one seek help if something goes wrong while locked into a hypnotic state?

New Age books

There are many publishing houses devoted to the NAM books, and there are hundreds of books available which claim to be NAM when they could be seen under a different classification, and vice versa. Usually these books are found under the classification of Philosophy/Religion/Occult in the bookshops. There is a danger, however, as many NAM books have Christian-sounding titles but, in fact, come from an occultic source, or from the dictations of channelled spirits. If they are from this source you will find subtle denials of Christian teaching in them. You will also find that Jesus of Nazareth, our Crucified and Risen Lord, is *not* referred to as THE CHRIST. He is spoken of as an enlightened man of his time, but that is all. We are more evolved nowadays, they claim, and must leave Christianity behind.

Many NAM books cover a wide range of subjects, and not all of the material is bad, but great discernment is needed in every case, as so many Christians have been led astray by reading them.

The crystal craze

All the writers on the NAM speak of the crystal craze as one of the most popular NAM things today, popular even with Christians! The belief in the power of crystals stems from the NAM belief that God is an impersonal force, or energy, which is vibrating in the Universe. If one wants to get into harmony with this energy then one may do so through certain objects that vibrate in harmony with this energy. NAM believes that crystal rocks, with their beautiful crystal shapes and patterns, vibrate with this energy. They believe that if you hold a crystal while meditating this energy will flow into you. One may even go further and focus deeply on a specific crystal in order to release psychic energy for psychic healing, contact with spirit entities, or in developing higher consciousness.

Elliot Miller says that crystals are used in a variety of therapies, such as psychic healing, acupuncture, 'dream work', aura and chakra cleansing and balancing.[6] Besides this they are used to enhance meditation, visualisation, astral or 'soul travel', channelling and various forms of divination. Many people also wear them as lucky charms, or to attract prosperity, the opposite sex, and so on. They appear to have endless functions!

Crystals are a modern form of using the old-fashioned magic charms and other occultic objects that missionaries found in use when they went to take Christianity to a new country or culture. Of course crystals, of themselves, have no power. They are merely beautiful stones. But when used with occultic ritual people experience power in association with them.[7]

Everyone accepts that they need help in meditation. The NAM first recommended TM and mantras; then this was not enough, you needed crystals. The latest craze is that you must sit under a pyramid! All these things belong to the same grouping, and indicate that people have turned away from God to what appears to be *anything* else.[8]

NAM and the work-place

A very difficult problem exists when NAM invades the work-place in the name of improved productivity and prosperity. Companies have now woken up to the fact that meditation techniques can help the work-force to unify, and to produce more and better quality work. So the question must be asked: Can these techniques be de-sacralised, that is, used without any religious content or overtones, as the NAM claims they can?

Elliot Miller has a very good discussion on this in his book *A Crash Course in the New Age*, pp. 98-102. He is speaking specifically about the American scene here, but many of the ideas are beginning to be used in Ireland also. The new language used for business seminars is TT, OD and OT among others. These are human potential seminars that promise greater motivation, 'vision' (to benefit the company), increased productivity and creativity (to benefit the company), improved teamwork and interpersonal skills, all of which should reduce absenteeism, and a lot of minor illness that disrupts the working and productivity of the company.

So, companies invite experts in Transpersonal technologies (TT) and the Movement for Inner Spiritual Awareness (MISA) to come along and transform the work-place. Once the individuals have been helped, then the company as a whole is helped by Organisational Development (OD) seminars which take them a step further in stress management for managers and employees, as well as interpersonal skills at different levels of the company. This in turn leads to OT training, in Organisational Transformation, where the company itself must see its place in the transformation of society, and develop its 'mission' in this field.

Here we have moved from planetising the individuals and groups within organisations to planetising the organisation itself. The methods used are typical of NAM. They consist of meditation, yoga, psychology, and all their related techniques. Miller says that the NAM leaders running these seminars met with practically no resistance because nobody believed that there *was* any connection with anything *but* the human mind involved.

Yet as we have already seen, it is not possible to de-sacralise these techniques. Instead, many people who have surrendered to these techniques report that they have ASCs and experience 'feelings of increased creativity, of *infinity*, and of *immortality;* they have *an evangelistic sense of mission* and report that both physical and mental sufferings vanish' (Miller, p. 94). Thus, instead of just relaxing, they have been baptised into psychic power and some are won over to the NAM itself, or to some other occultic grouping.

As Miller points out, the same things happen when these techniques are used in medicine to heal high blood pressure or other tension situations.

Miller quotes from the *New York Times* of 28 September 1986, which stated that 250 companies had admitted to using 'consciousness raising techniques', that these are the fastest type of executive development programmes in use. It also reported that the techniques used were meditation, chanting, dream work, the use of tarot cards and discussion of the 'New Age Capitalist'. Thirdly, it reported that executives from IBM, AT&T and General Motors met in New Mexico in July 1986 to discuss how metaphysics, the occult and Hindu mysticism could help their executives compete in the world market-place (p. 100).

There is nothing wrong in helping companies and their employees to function better as human beings, and as a group, but not at the price of their soul! Companies cannot presume to take over individuals as if they owned them. They have no right to impose a strange 'spirituality' on their employees just for the sake of prosperity, so great discernment is needed by the individuals involved. If this becomes commonplace here in Ireland, people will have to be alerted to their human rights to freedom of conscience, and freedom of decision regarding what techniques can be imposed on them in the name of productivity.

NOTES

1. For details of the Puja ceremony see John Allan, pp. 52-53. It involves the worship of Guru Dev, as well as the Hindu Pantheon. The TM mantra list is on pp. 55-56, showing that the so-called 'secret' mantra is given to everyone according to their age groups!

2. See also *TM Wants You* By David Haddon and Vail Hamilton 1976. This is a Christian response to TM, and deals with the subject thoroughly.

3. There is a very good discussion of the philosophical underpinnings of the system in the book: *Understanding Cults and New Religions*, Irving Hexam & Karla Poewe, Eerdman's, 1987, ch. 6. See also *Unicorn in The Sanctuary*, Randy England, 1990, pp. 40-45.

4. For more information see the video, *Gods of the New Age* by Jeremiah Films, which illustrates this very clearly.

5. See *Understanding Cults and New Religions*, 1987, p. 79. See also *What your Horoscope Doesn't Tell You*, Charles Stohmer, Word Publishing, 1988. This author is a former expert astrologer, who after some success with astrology decided to investigate its mysteries. He points out the occultic nature of this magical art, and agrees that there is nothing scientific about it.

6. In yogic philosophy the seven centres of spiritual energy in the body are called the chakras.

7. See *Inside the New Age Nightmare* 1989, Randall N. Baer, p. 106. See also *Unicorn in The Sanctuary*, Randy England, pp. 46-50, where he lists the uses of crystals. For example, you need quartz crystals to focus the energy of the body for harmony and balance; you need jade for wisdom, a sapphire to elevate your mood, etc.! Apparently Grace has become obsolete!

8. Russell Chandler discusses this fully in chapter 12 of his book *Understanding the New Age*.

SELECT BIBLIOGRAPHY

Revelation: The Birth of a New Age, David Spangler, Findhorn Foundation, Scotland, 1976. Second printing 1978.

Reimagination of the World, David Spangler and William Irwin, Thompson, Bear & Co., New Mexico, 1991.

The Secret Doctrine, Helena Blavatsky, Two volumes, the Theosophical Publishing Co., London, 1888.

The Reappearance of the Christ and the Masters of Wisdom, Benjamin Creme, Tara Press, London, 1979.

The Aquarian Conspiracy, Marilyn Ferguson, Paladin, Grafton Books, London, 1980, fifth reprinting 1988.

The Externalisation of the Hierarchy, Alice A. Bailey, Lucis Publishing Co., New York, London, 1957. Eighth printing 1989. The Lucis Trust controls a special Tibetan Book Fund for the perpetuation of the teachings of Alice Bailey. They are foundational teachings for the NAM.

The Rays and The Initiations, Alice A. Bailey, Lucis Publishing Co., New York,London, 1960. Seventh printing 1988.

The Planetary Commission, John Randolph Price, Quartus Foundation, Texas, 1984.

Understanding The New Age, Russell Chandler, Word Publishing, Milton Keynes,1989.

Dark Secrets of the New Age, Texe Marrs, Crossways Books, Illinois, 1987. Tenth printing 1988.

Inside The New Age Nightmare, Randall N. Baer, Huntington House Inc., Louisiana, 1989.

The Hidden Dangers of the Rainbow, Constance Cumbey, Huntington House Inc., Louisiana, 1983.

Straight Answers on the New Age, Bob Larson, Thomas Nelson Publishers, Nashville, Tennessee, 1989.

The Christian and The Supernatural, Morton T. Kelsey, Search Press, London, 1977.

Youth, Brainwashing and the Extremist Cults, Ronald Enroth, Paternoster Press, Grand Rapids, Michigan, 1977.

Confronting The New Age, Douglas Groothuis, Intervarsity Press, Downer's Grove, Illinois, 1988.

Unmasking The New Age, Douglas Groothuis, Intervarsity Press, Downer's Grove, Illinois, 1986.

A Crash Course in the New Age, Elliot Miller, Monarch Publishing, Eastbourne, Sussex, 1989.

Unicorn in the Sanctuary, Randy England, Trinity Communications, Manassas, VA, 1990.

The Beautiful Side of Evil, Johanna Michaelsen, Harvest House Publishers, Oregon, 1982.

The Secret Place, Richard E. McKenzie, Institute of Psychorientology, Texas, 1984.

Reflections:The Personal Evaluation by the Founder of Silva Mind Control, Jose Silva, Institute of Psychorientology, Texas 1979.

Beyond the Love Game, Robert Scheid, Celestial Arts, California,1980.

Understanding Cults and New Religions, Irving Hexam & Karla Poewe, Eerdmans Publishing Co., Grand Rapids, 1987.

TM Wants You! David Haddon & Vail Hamilton, Baker Books, Grand Rapids, 1976.

What Your Horoscope Doesn't Tell You, Charles Strohmer, Word Publishing, Milton Keynes, 1988.

Healing at any Price?, Samuel Pfeifer MD, Word Publishing, Milton Keynes, 1988.

The Challenging Counterfeit, Raphael Gasson, Bridge Publishing, UK, 1966. Eighteenth printing 1985.

TM: A Cosmic Confidence Trick, John Allen, Inter-Varsity Press, Leicester, 1980.